STOICISM FOR ADULTS WITH ADHD

KATHERINE SULLIVAN

Stoicism for Adults with ADHD © 2026 – Katherine Sullivan

ISBN: 978-91-89876-68-2

CHAPTER 1

Marcus Aurelius Probably Had ADHD

And what his private notebook reveals about the ADHD mind

Here is a man who commanded the most powerful empire on earth.

He had access to the best tutors, the most sophisticated philosophy, and arguably more power than any other human being alive at his time.

And yet, every single morning, he had to remind himself to get out of bed.

> *"At dawn, when you have trouble getting up, tell yourself: I have to go to work, as a human being. What do I have a complaint about, if I'm going to do what I was born for?"*
> — **Marcus Aurelius, Meditations**

Notice what he is doing. He is not inspiring himself. He is arguing with himself. He is almost annoyed with himself. That internal friction, that gap between knowing what to do and actually starting, is one of the most recognizable features of the ADHD experience.

The Meditations were never meant to be published. They were private notes, written to himself, during military campaigns.

Reminders. Arguments. Repeated over and over, as if writing them once was never enough.

Sound familiar?

The notebook nobody was supposed to read

The title Meditations is a bit misleading. In Greek, Marcus Aurelius called his notes Ta Eis Heauton, which roughly means Things to Oneself. It is a journal of self-corrections.

He circles back to the same ideas constantly. Do not waste time. Do not lose focus. Do not get pulled into other people's drama. Pay attention. Remember what matters. Get up. Work. Do not drift.

For most people, reading this feels like philosophy. For people with ADHD, it can feel like someone read your diary.

ADHD note

Executive dysfunction is the clinical term for the gap between intention and action. It is not a character flaw. It is a neurological feature. Marcus Aurelius described it in the second century. Neuroscience named it in the twentieth.

What the historical record suggests

We cannot diagnose someone who died 1,800 years ago. Any honest person will tell you that. But we can look at what he wrote and ask: does this pattern look familiar?

Here is what we know about Marcus Aurelius from historical sources:

- He struggled intensely with procrastination on tasks he found tedious, particularly administrative duties.
- He had periods of deep hyperfocus, especially during philosophical study.
- He wrote repeatedly about the need to manage his attention, as though it required constant external scaffolding.
- He was described as emotionally intense, compassionate to the point of sometimes being overwhelmed.
- He found mornings difficult throughout his life.
- He needed to write things down to make them feel real.

None of this proves anything. But here is the interesting part: whether Marcus Aurelius had ADHD or not does not actually matter for our purposes.

What matters is that a person who understood the human mind deeply enough to write one of history's great philosophical texts was also a person who had to work, every day, with a mind that did not simply cooperate.

He was not writing from a place of calm, centered wisdom. He was writing from the struggle.

That is why this philosophy works for you.

The problem with how stoicism gets taught today

If you have heard of stoicism before, you might picture a man in a suit talking about cold showers, discipline, and never complaining. Or you might picture a marble statue: serene, unmoved, above it all.

Neither of these is stoicism. Both of them are actively unhelpful for people with ADHD.

The modern stoic guru tends to present stoicism as a system for producing more output, tolerating more discomfort, and feeling less. That framing is both historically inaccurate and, frankly, exhausting.

Actual stoicism, as practiced by Marcus Aurelius, Epictetus, and Seneca, is about something much more interesting.

It is about learning to work with the nature you actually have, not the idealized nature you wish you had.

> *"You have power over your mind, not outside events. Realize this, and you will find strength."*
>
> — **Marcus Aurelius, Meditations**

For most people, this quote is about not being affected by setbacks. For someone with ADHD, it is about something more fundamental: recognizing that your mind is the thing you can actually work with, and your environment, your impulses, other people's expectations, those are not always within your power.

That reframe alone can lift an enormous weight.

What this book is and what it is not

This is not a book that will tell you stoicism will fix your ADHD. It will not. ADHD is a neurological difference, not a philosophical problem.

This is also not a book that will ask you to suppress how you feel, to push through without support, or to simply try harder.

What this book offers is a set of ideas, and a set of small practices, that are specifically useful for the kind of mind that thinks in bursts, feels everything deeply, loses track of time, and then suddenly produces something remarkable.

The stoics were not neuroscientists. But they were very good observers of the human mind. And some of what they observed is surprisingly specific to the ADHD experience.

We are going to go through their ideas one by one. We will connect each one to what modern neuroscience tells us about the ADHD brain. And at the end of each chapter, you will get a short, practical exercise. Nothing that takes more than two minutes. Nothing that requires you to be someone you are not.

Just tools. For your kind of mind.

YOUR PRACTICE

2-minute stoic exercises

Practice 1.1: The Marcus Aurelius Letter (2 minutes)

Marcus Aurelius wrote to himself. Constantly. It is how he kept his mind oriented.

Tonight, before you sleep or at the end of your day, write three sentences. That is all. You can do this on paper, on your phone, anywhere.

1. One thing I actually did today, no matter how small.
2. One moment I noticed my mind pulling me somewhere unhelpful.
3. One thing I want to remember tomorrow.

That is it. No journaling required. No reflection session. Three sentences.

Marcus Aurelius did this for decades. Not because it came naturally. Because it did not.

Practice 1.2: The morning argument (30 seconds)

When you find it hard to get up, try Marcus Aurelius's own script. Out loud or in your head:

> **Say this**
>
> I am going to do the thing I am here to do. It does not have to feel easy. It just has to happen.

Not motivational. Not inspiring. Just a statement of fact. Exactly how Marcus Aurelius used it.

If it feels silly to borrow words from a Roman emperor, remember: he was also talking to himself in an empty tent at 5am, trying to convince himself to get up. You are in good company.

CHAPTER 2

What Stoicism Is NOT

Clearing the debris before we build anything useful

Before we go any further, we need to have an honest conversation about what stoicism is not.

Because there is a version of stoicism circulating right now, especially online, that would be actively harmful for people with ADHD. And if that is the version you have encountered, it makes complete sense that you might be skeptical.

Let us go through the main myths one by one.

Myth 1: Stoicism means suppressing your emotions

This is the most common misunderstanding, and also the most damaging one.

The stoics did not ask you to stop feeling things. They were not trying to produce robots. Epictetus cried when his students left. Marcus Aurelius wrote about grief. Seneca, arguably the most human of all of them, wrote extensively about how emotions work and why trying to simply push them away is both ineffective and dishonest.

> *"It is not that I do not feel these things. It is that I do not let the feeling make the decision."*
> **— Seneca, Letters to Lucilius**

That is a completely different proposition. It is not about suppression. It is about creating a small gap between what you feel and what you do next.

For people with ADHD, that gap is precisely the challenge. Emotional responses tend to arrive fast and large. The amygdala, the brain's alarm system, fires more easily and more intensely in ADHD brains. The stoics were not asking you to silence the alarm. They were asking you to not immediately run out the door every time it goes off.

There is a word for that skill in modern psychology: affect regulation. The stoics called it working with your impressions. The mechanism is the same. We will spend a whole chapter on it.

ADHD note

Emotional dysregulation is one of the most underdiagnosed features of ADHD in adults. It is not in the official DSM criteria, which is why so many adults get missed. But research consistently shows it is one of the most impairing aspects of the condition.

Myth 2: Stoicism is about discipline and productivity

If you have seen stoicism marketed as a philosophy for high performers, elite athletes, or Silicon Valley entrepreneurs who wake up at 4am, you have seen it being sold as something it is not.

The original stoics were not productivity gurus. Marcus Aurelius was famously not interested in fame or legacy. Epictetus was a former slave who had almost nothing and considered himself among the most free of men. Seneca wrote a famous essay arguing that busyness itself, and the constant pursuit of more, was a kind of spiritual sickness.

> *"It is not that I have so much to do. It is that I lack a clear sense of what I am here for."*
> **— Seneca, On the Shortness of Life**

Stoicism is about clarity of values, not about output. That distinction matters enormously for ADHD.

ADHD already comes with a productivity narrative attached. You should be doing more. You should be keeping up. You should be as organized as that other person. Adding a stoic productivity overlay to that does not help. It piles expectation on top of shame.

The stoicism in this book is not about doing more. It is about knowing why you are doing anything at all.

Myth 3: Stoicism is about toughening up

There is a hyper-masculine thread in modern stoic content that has almost nothing to do with the original philosophy.

The real stoics were interested in self-compassion, though they did not use that word. Marcus Aurelius wrote explicitly about the danger of being too hard on yourself. Seneca argued that treating yourself with harshness was not virtue, it was a kind of pride in disguise.

More practically: for people with ADHD, self-criticism is already doing serious damage.

Research from Dr. Ned Hallowell and others who have worked extensively with ADHD populations suggests that by the time most people reach adulthood, they have received approximately 20,000 more critical comments than their non-ADHD peers. Twenty thousand more corrections. Redirections. Sighs. Disappointments.

The internal critic that results from that is not mild. It is constant, punishing, and often entirely out of proportion.

A stoicism that tells you to simply be tougher is not offering you philosophy. It is offering you more of the same thing that has already hurt you.

That is not what is in this book.

What we ARE doing

We are using stoic ideas, carefully selected, to build acceptance of how your mind works. Not resignation. Acceptance. There is a significant difference, and we will come back to it throughout the book.

Myth 4: Stoicism requires long, focused practice sessions

This one is almost funny, given the audience.

Real stoic practice was integrated into daily life. Marcus Aurelius wrote in short bursts during military campaigns. Epictetus taught in conversation. Seneca wrote letters. None of them were sitting in silent retreat for days at a time.

The practices in this book are short. Deliberately, unapologetically short. Two minutes or less. They are designed for a brain that does not reliably sustain attention on command, that thrives on novelty, and that needs variety in how it engages with ideas.

That is not a compromise. It is actually more faithful to how the stoics practiced than the long meditation sessions people sometimes imagine.

So what IS stoicism, actually?

At its core, stoicism is a practical philosophy built around one central insight: some things are up to you, and some things are not. Your job is to tell the difference, and to focus your energy accordingly.

That is it. Everything else in stoicism is an elaboration of that idea.

For people with ADHD, this insight lands differently than it does for others. Your attention, your emotions, your impulses, these do not always cooperate with your intentions. The ADHD brain is not a broken neurotypical brain. It is a different kind of brain, with its own features, its own strengths, and its own challenges.

Stoicism does not ask you to override those features. It asks you to understand what you can and cannot change, and to build your life around that honest assessment.

That is, genuinely, a more radical and more compassionate idea than anything in the productivity-stoic world.

A note on who the stoics were

Before we leave this chapter, a quick introduction to the people we will be spending time with:

- Marcus Aurelius (121 to 180 CE): Roman emperor, reluctant public figure, private philosopher. His Meditations is the book we will return to most.
- Epictetus (50 to 135 CE): Born into slavery, became one of the most influential philosophers in history. His Discourses and the Enchiridion are compact, sometimes blunt, always practical.
- Seneca (4 BCE to 65 CE): Playwright, politician, and the most human of the three. His Letters are personal, contradictory, and often surprisingly funny. He is also the one who wrote most extensively about emotions.

You do not need to have read any of their work to use this book. We will bring in what is useful, leave out what is not, and always connect it back to what the ADHD brain actually needs.

YOUR PRACTICE
2-minute stoic exercises

Practice 2.1: The myth check (1 minute)

Before going further in this book, take a moment to notice what you believed about stoicism before reading this chapter.

Pick the statement that most closely matched your assumption:

- Stoicism means not letting things affect you.
- Stoicism is for disciplined, high-achieving types.
- Stoicism is cold, intellectual, and distant.
- I had no idea what it was.

Write down which one you picked. Then write one sentence: what would have to be true for stoicism to be actually useful for me?

Keep that sentence somewhere you can find it. We will come back to it at the end of the book.

Practice 2.2: Spot the myth in the wild (ongoing)

This week, whenever you see stoicism mentioned, online, in a book title, in a quote, notice which version it is.

Is it the toughness version? The productivity version? The suppression version?

Or is it something closer to what we described here: working with what you actually have, understanding what is and is not in your control, building a life on honest values?

You do not need to do anything with this. Just notice. Noticing is where stoic practice begins.

CHAPTER 3

Your Brain is Not Broken. It's Calibrated Differently

What neuroscience tells us, and why it matters before we go any further

---

Before we get into stoic philosophy, we need to spend some time with your brain.

Not to fix it. Not to analyze everything that is hard. But because you cannot genuinely work with something you do not understand. And for a lot of people with ADHD, especially those who received a late diagnosis, the mental model of their own brain is still the one that was handed to them in childhood.

Which is, roughly: you are smart but lazy, you just need to try harder, and something is wrong with you.

None of that is accurate. Let us start over.

What ADHD actually is

ADHD, Attention Deficit Hyperactivity Disorder, is a neurodevelopmental condition affecting roughly 8 to 10 percent of children and 4 to 5 percent of adults worldwide. It is one of the most well-researched conditions in all of psychiatry.

The name is genuinely terrible, because it implies there is a deficit of attention. There is not. People with ADHD can focus intensely for hours on things they find interesting or urgent. What is actually going on is more interesting than a simple deficit.

The ADHD brain struggles to regulate attention. To direct it reliably toward things that are not intrinsically motivating or novel. Not to generate attention, but to deploy it on demand.

The key distinction

It is not that you cannot focus. It is that your brain's attention system runs on a different fuel. Neurotypical brains can fire attention based on intention alone. ADHD brains require interest, novelty, urgency, or challenge to engage reliably.

Dopamine and the ADHD brain

The central mechanism involves dopamine, and it is worth understanding even at a basic level.

Dopamine is a neurotransmitter involved in motivation, reward, and attention. In ADHD brains, dopamine signaling works differently. There is typically less tonic dopamine, the steady background level that makes routine tasks manageable, and a more dramatic phasic response to high-stimulation situations.

This explains several things that might have puzzled you about yourself:

- Why you can hyperfocus for six hours on something interesting but cannot do fifteen minutes of admin work.
- Why deadlines suddenly unlock your ability to function.

- Why you need music, background noise, or movement to concentrate.
- Why new projects feel electric and existing ones feel like wading through concrete.
- Why you keep seeking novelty even when you know the consequences.

None of these are character flaws. They are the behavioral expression of a brain with a particular dopamine profile.

> *"We are not dealing with a deficit of attention but with an inconsistency of access to it."*
> — **Dr. Russell Barkley, clinical psychologist and leading ADHD researcher**

Executive functions: the five things ADHD affects

Executive functions are the cognitive processes that manage goal-directed behavior. Think of them as the management layer of your brain. ADHD specifically impairs these.

The five most relevant for daily life are:

- Working memory: holding information in mind while using it. This is why you walk into a room and forget why, or lose the thread of a conversation.
- Inhibition: the ability to pause before acting or speaking. This is what feels like impulsivity, though it is more accurately described as a delay in the brake signal.

- Emotional regulation: the ability to modulate the intensity of emotional responses. ADHD does not make you more emotional, it makes the experience of emotion more immediate and harder to buffer.
- Time perception: sensing how long things take and how much time has passed. The ADHD experience of time is often described as only two modes: now and not now.
- Planning and prioritization: breaking tasks into sequences and deciding what to do first. This is where the paralysis lives.

We will come back to all of these throughout the book, because each one has a stoic concept that maps onto it in useful ways.

> **This is important**
>
> Knowing which executive function is struggling in a given moment changes everything. It means you can respond specifically instead of just feeling generically overwhelmed. We will build that skill chapter by chapter.

The shame accumulation problem

Here is something that is rarely discussed in books about ADHD, and it needs to be said clearly.

By the time most people with ADHD reach adulthood, especially those who were diagnosed late or not at all, they have accumulated an enormous amount of shame.

Not because they failed. Because they succeeded, and it still was not enough. Because they tried harder than anyone around them and still got the same criticism. Because they developed elaborate systems and then forgot to use them. Because they promised things and then could not deliver, not because they did not care, but because their brain could not reliably translate caring into action.

That accumulation does not announce itself as shame. It disguises itself as:

- Avoiding tasks you are actually capable of.
- Not starting things because you are afraid of not finishing.
- Saying yes when you mean maybe, because admitting uncertainty feels dangerous.
- Feeling fraudulent when things go well.
- Expecting criticism even when it is not coming.

Stoicism is not a cure for this. But it offers something important: a framework that starts from acceptance of reality rather than a gap between who you are and who you should be.

The stoics were very clear that you cannot work from a false picture of your situation. You have to start with what is actually true.

And what is actually true is: your brain is not broken. It is calibrated differently. Some environments will never work well for it. Some tasks will always cost you more than they cost others. That is real, and it deserves to be acknowledged as real.

It also means that many of the strategies, systems, and advice you have received in your life were not designed for your brain. Of course they did not work. They were not built for you.

This book is.

What ADHD looks like when it is working with you

We have spent this chapter on the challenges, because you need an accurate map. But no honest chapter about the ADHD brain ends without acknowledging the other side.

The same neurological features that make certain tasks disproportionately hard also produce things that are genuinely valuable:

- Pattern recognition that happens faster than deliberate thinking.
- Creative leaps that bypass the steps other people get stuck on.
- Intense empathy and emotional attunement.
- Hyperfocus that, when it lands on the right thing, produces extraordinary work.
- Genuine novelty-seeking that drives innovation.
- A tendency to ask why that irritates bureaucracies and advances knowledge.

The stoics would say: this is your nature. Work with it, not against it. Build a life that fits it rather than one that demands you be something else.

That is exactly what we are going to do.

YOUR PRACTICE
2-minute stoic exercises

Practice 3.1: Name the executive function (ongoing, 1 minute each time)

This week, when you notice yourself struggling, try to name which executive function is involved. Be specific.

Instead of
I am useless at this. >> Try: My working memory is struggling right now. My inhibition system is offline. My time perception has gone sideways.

This is not about excusing anything. It is about accuracy. You cannot fix a vague problem. You can work with a specific one.

At the end of each day this week, write down one specific moment and which executive function was involved. Just one. Takes sixty seconds.

Practice 3.2: The accurate mirror (2 minutes)

Write down two lists. Be honest with both.

Things that cost me more than they cost most people:

1. (your own entry)
2. (your own entry)
3. (your own entry)

Things I do that genuinely come from how my brain works well:

1. (your own entry)
2. (your own entry)
3. (your own entry)

The stoics called this knowing yourself accurately. Not the idealized self, not the criticized self. The real one.

This list is not a performance review. It is a map. You will need it for everything that comes next.

Practice 3.3: The reframe card (keep it somewhere visible)

Write this down and put it somewhere you will see it regularly. On your phone. On a sticky note. On your bathroom mirror.

When I struggle, I say:
This is not a character flaw. This is a specific executive function under strain. I can work with this.

Not instead of getting help. Not as a substitute for strategies. But as the baseline: accurate, kind, and honest.

That is where stoic practice begins.

CHAPTER 4

The One Stoic Idea You Actually Need

The dichotomy of control, and why it hits differently when you have ADHD

If you only take one idea from this entire book, let it be this one.

The stoics built their entire philosophy on a single distinction. Everything in their system, every practice, every piece of advice, every observation about human suffering, flows from this one insight.

Some things are up to you. Some things are not.

That is it. The whole thing. The rest is detail.

Epictetus, who wrote about this more directly than anyone, called it the dichotomy of control. He opened his most famous work, the Enchiridion, with it. Not as a warm-up. As the entire point.

> *"Some things are in our control and others not. Things in our control are opinion, pursuit, desire, aversion, and, in a word, whatever are our own actions. Things not in our control are body, reputation, command, and, in one word, whatever are not our own actions."*
>
> **— Epictetus, Enchiridion**

Read that list again. Body. Reputation. What other people think. The outcomes of your efforts. None of those are in your control, according to Epictetus.

Only your own responses, judgments, and choices are yours.

For most people this is a useful philosophical reminder. For people with ADHD, it can be something closer to a rescue line.

Why this lands differently for ADHD brains

Here is the thing about growing up with ADHD, especially undiagnosed: you spend years believing that the things outside your control are your fault.

You forget things. You are late. You lose objects. You cannot finish what you start. You react too strongly. You make the same mistake twice, then three times, then again, even though you genuinely meant not to.

And the message you receive, from school, from family, from your own internal critic, is that this is a character problem. A motivation problem. A trying-hard-enough problem.

It is not. And the dichotomy of control gives you a framework for being precise about why.

The honest map

Things genuinely in your control: how you respond to difficulty, the systems you put in place, whether you ask for help, how you talk to yourself after a mistake, the values you choose to act from. Things not fully in your control: whether your attention cooperates on demand, how your brain processes time, how your emotions arrive, other people's reactions to your ADHD.

That second list is not an excuse. It is a fact. And facts are where useful work begins.

Once you stop spending energy blaming yourself for things that were never fully in your control, you have more energy available for the things that actually are.

The trap: using control as an excuse

Before we go further, a necessary warning. The dichotomy of control is not a permission slip to stop trying.

Epictetus was the furthest thing from passive. He was a former slave who built a school of philosophy. He was relentlessly demanding of his students, and of himself.

The point of distinguishing what is and is not in your control is not to give up on the things outside it. It is to stop measuring your worth by them, and to redirect your energy toward what you can actually influence.

You cannot control whether your brain initiates a task easily. You can control whether you design your environment to lower the threshold for starting. That is a meaningful distinction.

You cannot control the emotional intensity that arrives when you are overwhelmed. You can control, over time and with practice, how quickly you respond to it.

The goal is precision, not passivity.

The ADHD version of this practice

Most people who encounter the dichotomy of control apply it to big things. Career setbacks. Relationship problems. Health worries.

For ADHD, the more useful application is granular and daily. Because the ADHD experience involves dozens of small moments each day where the line between what is and is not in your control gets blurry.

You lose your keys. Is that your fault? Partly, in that you did not put them in their designated place. But also partly not, in that the working memory challenges of ADHD make automatic habituation genuinely harder than it is for other people.

Both things can be true. You are not a victim of your brain. And your brain also makes certain things harder. The stoic move is to hold both simultaneously and ask: given this reality, what is the one thing I can actually do here?

> *"Make the best use of what is in your power, and take the rest as it happens."*
> — **Epictetus, Enchiridion**

That is the entire instruction. Make the best use of what is in your power. Not what you wish were in your power. Not what should be in your power if you were a different kind of person. What actually is.

A word about effort and fairness

People with ADHD often expend more effort than those around them to achieve the same results. A task that takes a neurotypical colleague thirty minutes might take you two hours, with a full emotional aftermath.

That is not fair. And stoicism does not pretend otherwise. The stoics were clear-eyed about the fact that life distributes advantages unevenly. What they offered was not comfort, but usefulness: given the hand you have been dealt, what is the wisest move?

The dichotomy of control does not tell you that everything is fine. It tells you where to put your attention so that things can get better.

That is a more honest kind of help than most books offer.

YOUR PRACTICE
2-minute stoic exercises

Practice 4.1: The two-column sort (2 minutes)

When something is bothering you today, write it at the top of a piece of paper. Then draw a line down the middle.

Left column: what is not in my control about this.

Right column: what is in my control about this.

Be honest about both sides. The left column is not an excuse. The right column is not a demand. It is just a map.

Do this once a day for one week. Not for every problem. Just one thing, each day. The habit of sorting is more valuable than any single sort.

Practice 4.2: The granular pause (30 seconds, as needed)

When you catch yourself in a spiral, whether it is self-criticism, frustration, or anxiety, try one question:

Ask yourself

Is what I am upset about something I can actually change right now, or am I spending energy on something that was never mine to control?

You do not need to answer perfectly. The pause alone disrupts the spiral.

Epictetus called this checking your impressions. You are not suppressing the feeling. You are asking whether the story attached to it is accurate.

Practice 4.3: The effort reframe (ongoing)

When you notice yourself comparing your output or performance to someone else's, try this substitution:

Instead of: they did it faster and easier, so I am failing.

Try: they have a different starting point. My job is to do what I can from mine.

That is not lowering the bar. That is setting the right bar. The one that is actually yours.

CHAPTER 5

The Distracted Pilot

Hegemonikon, executive control, and the part of you that keeps trying

---

The stoics believed that inside every human mind there was something they called the hegemonikon.

The word is Greek. It means the ruling part, or the leading faculty. Think of it as the pilot of the mind. The part that observes, evaluates, makes decisions, and directs action.

Not the emotions. Not the impulses. Not the habits. The part that watches all of those and, in theory, steers.

In theory.

The pilot with a noisy cockpit

For people with ADHD, the hegemonikon, or whatever we choose to call that executive faculty, is present and functional. It is not missing. It has not been replaced by something worse.

But it is working in conditions that make the job significantly harder.

Imagine a pilot who is competent, trained, and genuinely trying to fly the plane. But the cockpit is louder than everyone else's. The instruments flicker. Some alerts fire at random. There are twice as many incoming signals as the standard cockpit, and no reliable way to mute the irrelevant ones.

That pilot is not incompetent. They are dealing with a different set of conditions than the pilots around them.

That is the ADHD experience of executive function.

> **What neuroscience adds**
>
> The prefrontal cortex, the region of the brain most associated with executive control, inhibition, and planning, develops more slowly in ADHD brains and operates with less consistent dopamine signaling. This does not mean it cannot function. It means it requires more deliberate scaffolding to function reliably.

What the hegemonikon actually does

For the stoics, the hegemonikon had one primary job: evaluating impressions.

An impression, in stoic terms, is anything that arrives in your mind. A thought. An emotion. An impulse. A perception. The hegemonikon's role is to receive these, examine them, and decide how to respond.

That process, in modern psychology, is roughly what we mean by inhibitory control: the ability to pause between stimulus and response.

This is the executive function that ADHD most directly impairs.

And this is where stoicism becomes not just philosophically interesting but practically useful. Because the stoics spent centuries developing techniques for strengthening exactly this capacity.

Not through willpower. Through practice. Specific, repeatable, small-scale practice.

The observer is always there

Here is something important that often gets lost in descriptions of ADHD: the observing self is intact.

Most people with ADHD can describe, in precise and often painful detail, exactly what they were doing when they got distracted, why they did not start the task, what the spiral felt like as it was happening. The self-awareness is there.

What is missing is not awareness. It is the reliable connection between awareness and action.

The stoics would say: your hegemonikon is working. Your capacity to observe, to judge, to want to do better, all of that is functional. The challenge is building the habits and structures that help it act on what it sees.

That is a much more accurate and much more hopeful description of the ADHD situation than the standard narrative of deficit and failure.

> *"You have power over your mind, not outside events. Realize this, and you will find strength."*
> **— Marcus Aurelius, Meditations**

The power Marcus Aurelius is talking about is not the power to make your brain cooperate on demand. It is the power to keep returning to the attempt. To notice when you have drifted, and come back. To try again after the tenth failure with roughly the same commitment as after the first.

That capacity, the capacity to keep returning, is something ADHD brains often have in abundance. It tends to look like stubbornness from the outside. From the inside, it is something closer to faith in the attempt.

Building the pilot's instruments

The stoics were very practical about this. They did not believe that the hegemonikon strengthened itself through good intentions alone. They believed it required daily exercise.

Their exercises were small and consistent. A morning review of what lay ahead. An evening reflection on what had gone well and what had not. A practice of noticing, in real time, when an impression had been accepted without examination.

For ADHD brains, these practices need modification. Not because the ideas are wrong, but because the delivery system matters enormously. A practice that requires twenty minutes of quiet focus will fail. A practice that takes two minutes and can be done while walking will stick.

The goal in every case is the same: to strengthen the connection between the observing self and the choosing self. To reduce the gap between noticing that you have drifted and actually returning.

Every time you notice you have drifted and come back, you have done the work. Not failed. Done the work.

A note on self-criticism after distraction

One of the most counterproductive habits in the ADHD experience is the extended self-criticism session that follows a period of distraction.

You lose twenty minutes to a rabbit hole. Then you spend another ten minutes telling yourself what a disaster you are. Net result: thirty minutes lost, plus a dopamine crash that makes returning to work even harder.

The stoics had a direct response to this pattern. Marcus Aurelius wrote about it explicitly: when you fail to act as you intended, note it, understand why, and return to the attempt. Do not add suffering to the failure.

The hegemonikon does not become stronger through punishment. It becomes stronger through practice. Those are different things.

The stoic rule after a drift

Notice. Return. No commentary required. The noticing is the practice. The return is the practice. The self-criticism that follows is not practice. It is noise.

YOUR PRACTICE

2-minute stoic exercises

Practice 5.1: Count the returns (ongoing)

Today, every time you notice you have drifted from what you intended, and you return to it, count it.

Not the drifts. The returns.

At the end of the day, that number is your score. Each return is a rep. You are strengthening the connection between the observer and the actor. The drifts are irrelevant to the score.

Most people with ADHD find that they return dozens of times on a normal day. That is not a failure statistic. That is a training volume most neurotypical people never approach.

Practice 5.2: The three-breath return (30 seconds)

When you notice you have drifted, before doing anything else, take three slow breaths. Then ask one question:

The return question

What was I actually trying to do before I drifted? Not why did I drift. Not what is wrong with me. Just: what was I doing?

Answer that question, and go back to it. That is the entire practice.

The stoics called this returning to your ruling faculty. Modern psychology calls it redirecting attention. The mechanism is identical. The breath is there to create the gap that ADHD tends to close.

Practice 5.3: Evening pilot review (2 minutes)

Before sleep, three questions. Write them or just think them.

- When did I notice myself drifting today and manage to return?
- What made it easier to return in that moment?
- What is one thing I want my pilot to focus on tomorrow?

Marcus Aurelius did a version of this every night. Not because he was naturally disciplined. Because he was not, and he knew it.

CHAPTER 6

Pausing Before You React

Phantasia, the 3-second gap, and why your ADHD brain isn't the enemy

---

Every thought that arrives in your mind, every emotion, every urge, every perception, the stoics called these impressions. In Greek: phantasia.

And they made a distinction that most people in the ancient world, and honestly most people today, completely miss.

They said: an impression is not the same as a judgment about the impression.

Something happens. That is the impression. Then you decide what it means and what to do about it. That is the judgment. And between those two things, even if only for a fraction of a second, there is a gap.

Stoic practice is largely about learning to live in that gap.

The ADHD gap problem

For most people, the gap between impression and response is small but present. For people with ADHD, it can feel like it does not exist at all.

Someone says something mildly critical. The response arrives before the thought has finished forming. You send the message before you have read it twice. You say yes before you have checked your calendar. You push back before you have fully heard the other person's point.

This is not weakness. It is neurological. The inhibitory control system in ADHD brains is slower and less reliable. The gap does not close automatically. It requires active, practiced effort to stay open.

But here is the thing: the gap can be trained. Not perfectly. Not every time. But meaningfully, over time, with the right kind of practice.

And the stoics figured out how to train it almost two thousand years before neuroscience confirmed why it was necessary.

> **What the research says**
>
> Inhibitory control, the ability to pause a prepotent response, is one of the core executive functions most directly impaired by ADHD. It is also one of the most trainable, not through willpower, but through repeated practice of specific pause techniques in low-stakes situations.

The stoic technique: checking your impressions

Epictetus taught his students to do something simple but radical. When an impression arrived, before acting on it, he told them to pause and ask: is this impression something I should assent to?

Assent is a technical term in stoic philosophy. It means the moment when you accept an impression as true and decide to act on it. The stoics believed that assent was always, in principle, voluntary. Even if it did not feel that way.

Even if the impression arrived fast, and loud, and with a strong emotional charge attached to it.

The practice was not to reject the impression. It was to look at it first before deciding what to do with it.

> *"First say to yourself what you would be, and then do what you have to do."*
> **— Epictetus, Discourses**

In modern terms: know your intention before you act. Even a one-second intention check changes the quality of the action.

For ADHD, a one-second intention check is genuinely hard. Three seconds is a stretch goal. But it is also, once practiced, completely achievable. And three seconds is enough.

The emotional intensity factor

One of the specific challenges of ADHD is that impressions do not arrive at moderate volume. They tend to arrive at full intensity.

Frustration does not arrive as mild irritation. It arrives as rage. Embarrassment does not arrive as mild discomfort. It arrives as shame. Excitement does not arrive as pleasant interest. It arrives as obsession.

This is sometimes called emotional amplification, and it is one of the least discussed features of ADHD. The emotional experience is not disproportionate in the sense of being unreal. The feelings are real. But they are louder than the situation typically warrants.

The stoics were clear that this kind of amplification is where most of the damage happens. Not in the original impression, but in the runaway judgment that attaches to it.

Someone is late to a meeting. That is the impression. Then comes the amplified judgment: they do not respect my time, they never have, this always happens, I knew this relationship was a problem. And suddenly you are responding not to a late colleague but to a story you built in approximately four seconds.

You are not the impression

This is the most important distinction the stoics made, and it maps almost perfectly onto what neuroscience now tells us about the ADHD experience.

The impression is not you. The emotion is not you. The impulse is not you. They are things that arise in you. That is not a minor difference.

If you identify with every thought and feeling that passes through your mind, then when your ADHD brain produces a flood of competing impulses, you are those impulses. You are the chaos.

If you learn to see thoughts and impulses as things that arise in the mind, rather than things that are the mind, then you are the observer. And the observer, as we discussed in the last chapter, is steadier than the weather passing through.

The stoics spent a lot of time on this. Marcus Aurelius wrote about it in almost every section of the Meditations. Epictetus made it the foundation of his teaching.

They kept returning to it because it is genuinely difficult. And because it is genuinely necessary.

A useful image

Think of your mind as a sky. Thoughts, impulses, and emotions are the weather. You are the sky, not the storm. The storm arrives. The storm passes. The sky was there before it and will be there after.

Practicing the gap when everything is calm

The worst time to practice pausing is in the middle of an emotional spike. That is too late. The gap needs to be trained when the stakes are low, so it becomes available when the stakes are high.

This is the stoic insight that maps most directly onto modern behavioral psychology. You practice the pause in safe conditions. You practice it until it becomes a habit. Then it is there, at least partly, when you need it.

Not always. Not perfectly. But more than it would have been without practice.

That is the bar. Not perfection. More than before.

YOUR PRACTICE

2-minute stoic exercises

Practice 6.1: The 3-second rule (ongoing)

Choose one recurring situation in your life where you tend to react before you think. It could be a type of email. A particular person. A specific trigger at home or work.

This week, when that situation arrives, your only job is to pause for three seconds before responding.

Not to respond perfectly. Not to feel calm. Just to pause for three seconds.

Three seconds is enough to

Let the first wave of the impulse pass. Check whether you actually want to say or do what you were about to say or do. Decide instead of react.

Start with one situation. One. Not all of them. The practice builds from specific to general, not the other way around.

Practice 6.2: Name the impression (1 minute)

When a strong emotion or impulse arrives, try naming it before acting on it. Out loud or in writing.

Not: I am furious.

But: Anger has arrived. Or: I am noticing an impulse to respond sharply.

The grammatical shift matters. Moving from I am to I am noticing creates the observer's perspective. You are not the weather. You are watching the weather.

Research in emotion regulation confirms this. Labeling an emotion with some distance reduces its intensity measurably. The stoics knew this and practiced it as a matter of course.

Practice 6.3: The phantom review (2 minutes, end of day)

At the end of the day, think of one moment where a strong impression arrived. Walk through it in three steps:

- What was the impression? Describe it without judgment.
- What did you do with it? Be honest.
- If you could insert a three-second gap next time, what might you choose instead?

This is not self-criticism. This is the pilot doing a post-flight review. Same information, different purpose. The goal is to learn the terrain, not to punish the last flight.

Marcus Aurelius did this every evening. He called it examining the day. He was not always happy with what he found. He kept examining anyway.

CHAPTER 7

Impulse as Information

Why your impulses are not the enemy, and what they are actually trying to tell you

---

There is a version of the ADHD story that goes like this: your impulses are the problem. They get you in trouble. They interrupt people, spend money you do not have, send messages you regret, pull you away from what you were supposed to be doing.

Control the impulses, the story goes, and you control the ADHD.

That story is not entirely wrong, but it is missing something important. And what it is missing is this: impulses are not random noise. They are signals. And before you learn to manage them, it helps enormously to understand what they are actually saying.

What the stoics understood about desire and aversion

The stoics had a sophisticated model of the inner life that is remarkably close to what modern psychology has pieced together over the past fifty years.

They divided all inner movements into two categories: desire, the pull toward something, and aversion, the push away from something. Every impulse, they said, belongs to one of these two families.

And here is the insight that most people skip over: every desire and every aversion is pointing at something you value.

You interrupt someone because you value being heard. You avoid the task because you fear confirming something you believe about yourself. You seek novelty because your brain genuinely needs stimulation to function. You spend impulsively because the object represents relief from a feeling you cannot name.

The impulse is not the problem. The impulse is data. The question is whether you are reading it accurately.

> *"Seek not that the things which happen should happen as you wish, but wish the things which happen to be as they are, and you will have a tranquil flow of life."*
> — **Epictetus, Enchiridion**

This is often read as passive acceptance. It is not. It is an instruction to start with reality before you try to change it. And reality, in this case, includes the reality of what your impulses are telling you about what you need.

The ADHD impulse is louder, not wronger

One of the cruelest things about the standard framing of ADHD impulsivity is that it treats every impulse as suspect. As something to be suppressed rather than understood.

But the content of ADHD impulses is not irrational. The volume is high. The timing is often poor. The expression can be clumsy. But underneath almost every impulsive behavior, there is a legitimate need that is not being met through conventional channels.

The person who cannot stop talking in a meeting is often someone whose brain has made a connection that feels genuinely urgent and that will be gone if they do not say it now. The person who walks out of a boring situation is often someone whose nervous system is genuinely, physiologically understimulated. The person who buys something they cannot afford is often someone trying to create a dopamine event because their baseline dopamine is too low to sustain focus or motivation.

None of this makes the behavior consequence-free. But it makes it comprehensible. And comprehensible is where change becomes possible.

The reframe

An impulsive action is not evidence of a broken character. It is evidence of an unmet need that found the fastest available exit. Your job is not to seal all the exits. It is to build better ones.

Reading the signal under the impulse

The stoics recommended a practice they called examining desire: when you notice a strong pull toward or away from something, pause and ask what value is underneath it.

For ADHD, this is a genuinely useful skill. Not because it will stop the impulse in the moment, but because over time it builds a map of your actual needs. And once you have that map, you can start to meet those needs in ways that do not create problems.

Here is what that looks like in practice. You notice an impulse to check your phone for the fifteenth time in an hour. Instead of just doing it, or just feeling guilty about it, you pause for three seconds and ask: what am I actually looking for right now?

Sometimes the answer is stimulation. Sometimes it is connection. Sometimes it is avoidance of a task that feels threatening. Sometimes it is genuine boredom that your brain is signaling needs addressing.

Each of those answers points to a different response. Stimulation can be addressed by changing your environment. Connection can be addressed by a two-minute conversation with someone. Avoidance of a threatening task is worth understanding. Boredom is your nervous system telling you the current situation is not providing enough input.

None of those are fixed by putting your phone down and white-knuckling through. They are fixed by understanding what is actually happening and addressing it directly.

The difference between indulging and understanding

A necessary clarification: reading your impulse as information is not the same as acting on it.

The stoics were careful here. Understanding that a desire points at something you value does not mean the desire should be satisfied. It means you have enough information to make a deliberate choice rather than an automatic one.

Sometimes you will examine the impulse, understand what it is saying, and still decide not to act on it because the consequences are not worth it. That is a fundamentally different experience than suppressing the impulse through shame or willpower.

One exhausts you. The other, over time, builds something like genuine agency. Which is, of course, exactly what the stoics were after.

> *"He who is not satisfied with a little, is satisfied with nothing."*
> **— Epictetus, Fragments**

What Epictetus is pointing at is not deprivation. It is the difference between acting from clarity about what you genuinely need versus acting from a craving that has taken over the steering wheel.

For ADHD brains, where cravings arrive fast and loud, that distinction is everything.

Your impulses are not your identity

One more thing, and it matters.

Many people with ADHD, especially those who have been criticized for their impulsivity for years, have come to identify with their impulses. They think of themselves as impulsive people. As people who cannot control themselves.

The stoic view is more precise than that. You are not your impulses. You are the faculty that receives them, examines them, and chooses what to do next. The impulses arise. They pass. They tell you things. You decide what to do with what they tell you.

That is the observer again, the hegemonikon from the last chapter. It is there. It is watching. And it is not the same as the impulse.

That gap between the impulse and the choice is small. For ADHD brains, it is sometimes vanishingly small. But it exists. And it is yours.

YOUR PRACTICE
2-minute stoic exercises

Practice 7.1: The impulse interview (2 minutes)

When you notice a strong impulse today, before acting on it or suppressing it, try a quick three-question interview. You can do this in your head, in thirty seconds.

- What is this impulse pulling me toward, or pushing me away from?
- What need or value is underneath it? What is it actually trying to get for me?
- Is there a better way to meet that need right now?

You do not need to answer perfectly. The habit of asking is more valuable than any single answer. Over a week of this practice, you will start to notice patterns in your impulses that you could not see before.

Practice 7.2: The impulse log (ongoing, 1 minute per entry)

Keep a running note on your phone this week. Every time you catch a significant impulse, jot down three things:

1. What the impulse was.
2. What you think was underneath it.
3. What you actually did.

No judgment. No scoring. Just data. At the end of the week, read back through it and look for patterns. Most people find two or three recurring needs that their impulses are consistently pointing at. Those are the things worth addressing directly.

Practice 7.3: Build a better exit (once this week)

Pick one recurring impulse that tends to cause problems. The phone checking. The interrupting. The avoidance. The spending. Whatever yours is.

Ask: what need is this meeting? Then ask: what is one other way I could meet that need that does not create the same consequences?

> **Example**
>
> Impulse: checking social media repeatedly. Underlying need: stimulation and a sense of connection. Better exit: a two-minute walk, or a quick message to someone I actually want to talk to.

You are not eliminating the need. You are building a door that leads somewhere better. That is not self-control. That is self-knowledge. And self-knowledge is more durable.

CHAPTER 8

Meditating Without Sitting Still

What stoic contemplative practice actually looked like, and why it was never about the lotus position

---

When most people hear the word meditation, they picture someone sitting very still, eyes closed, doing something calm and focused for at least twenty minutes.

If you have ADHD, you probably also picture the version where you try this, spend nineteen of those twenty minutes planning what to have for dinner and feeling guilty about it, and then conclude that meditation is not for you.

Here is the good news: that is not stoic meditation. Not even close.

The stoics meditated by walking. By writing. By talking out loud to themselves. By reviewing the day while getting dressed. By asking questions during a meal. Their practice was woven into the texture of daily life, not separated from it into a dedicated session that requires stillness and silence.

If you have a brain that does not reliably sit still, you are actually much closer to how the stoics actually practiced than the modern meditation industry would have you believe.

What stoic contemplation actually was

The stoics used several specific contemplative practices. None of them require a cushion.

The morning review was perhaps the most common. Before the day began, the stoic would briefly consider what lay ahead. Not to plan obsessively, but to orient. What challenges might arise today? Where might I be tempted to react badly? What do I want to bring to this?

Marcus Aurelius did this. Epictetus taught it. Seneca described it in his letters. The review was short, practical, and done in ordinary conditions, often while still in bed, or over breakfast, or walking to wherever the day was taking them.

> **A stoic morning review takes two minutes**
> Think of one thing that might be difficult today. Not to worry about it. Just to see it coming. Then ask: what is the one quality I want to bring to that moment? That is the whole practice.

The evening reflection was the other anchor. At the end of the day, the stoic would run a brief audit of what had happened. Not a self-flagellation session. An honest look.

Seneca described this clearly in his letters: he would ask himself three questions before sleep. Where did I go wrong? Where did I do well? Where could I have done better?

Notice the order. Where did I go wrong comes first, but it is not the only question, and it is not followed by a verdict. It is followed by where I did well. The tone is that of a coach reviewing footage, not a judge delivering a sentence.

Walking as a contemplative practice

The Peripatetics, a different school of ancient philosophy, were famous for thinking while walking. Their name literally means those who walk around. But the stoics also valued movement as a context for reflection.

For ADHD brains, this is not just philosophically legitimate. It is neurologically supported.

Physical movement increases dopamine and norepinephrine, two of the neurotransmitters most directly implicated in ADHD. A ten-minute walk does not just help you think. It literally improves the conditions in which your executive functions operate. The stoics were onto something that neuroscience has now confirmed from the other direction.

If you find it impossible to sit and reflect, try walking and reflecting. The same questions work. The same practices work. You just do them in motion.

> *"Retire into yourself as much as you can. Associate with people who are likely to improve you."*
> **— Seneca, Letters to Lucilius**

Retiring into yourself does not mean sitting in a quiet room. It means creating moments of inner attention. Those moments can happen on a walk, in a shower, during a commute, while doing dishes. The container matters much less than the practice.

Writing as stoic meditation

Marcus Aurelius's entire legacy is a written contemplative practice. The Meditations were not polished essays. They were the raw material of a man thinking on paper, returning to the same questions, working through the same difficulties, catching himself drifting and noting it down.

For many people with ADHD, writing is the most effective form of reflection. Not journaling in the elaborate, daily-pages sense. Just brief, honest writing.

Three sentences. Five bullets. One question and an attempt at an answer. The act of converting the noise in your head into words on a page does something that thinking alone cannot reliably do: it slows the stream enough to see what is in it.

This is particularly valuable for ADHD brains, where thoughts tend to arrive in clusters and depart before they can be examined. Writing catches them.

Contemplation without perfectionism

One of the most common ways people with ADHD abandon contemplative practices is through the perfectionism trap. They miss one morning review and conclude the practice has failed. They do a rushed, distracted evening reflection and decide it does not count.

The stoics would find this baffling. Marcus Aurelius wrote in the Meditations about returning to the practice after interruption, not about maintaining an unbroken streak. Seneca explicitly said that a good practice done imperfectly is better than a perfect practice never attempted.

The bar is not consistency. The bar is return. When you drift from the practice, which you will, because everyone does, the question is simply: how quickly can I come back?

That is the same question as chapter five. The pilot returning to the controls. It is always the same question. The practice just gives you more opportunities to practice the return.

The only rule

A two-minute practice done six days a week beats a twenty-minute practice done once a month. Not because of the minutes. Because the six-day practice is building a habit. The once-a-month practice is maintaining an aspiration. Those are different things.

The practice that fits your brain

Different people with ADHD find different formats work better for them. There is no universal correct delivery system. What matters is that the practice happens, not how it looks.

Some people do their best reflecting while driving. Some use voice memos. Some write in apps on their phone. Some keep a physical notebook by the bed. Some do it while exercising. Some talk through their review out loud in the shower because the sound of running water helps their nervous system settle.

All of these are valid. All of them are, in their own way, exactly what the stoics did. The format is not the practice. The intention is the practice.

Find yours. Protect it. Come back to it when you lose it. That is everything.

YOUR PRACTICE
2-minute stoic exercises

Practice 8.1: The two-minute morning orient (daily)

Before you look at your phone or start any task, ask yourself two questions. Out loud, in your head, or written down, whatever works.

- What is the one thing most likely to be difficult today?
- What quality do I want to bring to it?

That is the whole practice. It takes ninety seconds. It does not require stillness, silence, or even sitting down. Marcus Aurelius did a version of this in a military tent. You can do it in bed.

Practice 8.2: The Seneca evening audit (daily, 2 minutes)

Before sleep, three questions in whatever form works for you. Written, spoken, or just thought:

- Where did I go wrong today? Just one thing, honestly named.
- Where did I do well? Just one thing, genuinely acknowledged.
- What do I want to do differently tomorrow?

No elaboration required. No perfect answers. Just the honest scan. Seneca said this practice alone, done consistently, changes the quality of how you move through your days.

He was right. But only if you actually do it.

Practice 8.3: The walking question (as needed)

When you are stuck, overwhelmed, or spinning, instead of sitting and trying to think your way out, take a ten-minute walk with one question in your head.

Good walking questions

What is actually bothering me right now, underneath the surface? What is the one thing I could do today that would make everything else easier? What would I tell a friend in exactly this situation?

Do not force an answer. Walk with the question. The answer often arrives without being chased.

This is not magical thinking. This is dopamine mechanics. Movement changes your neurochemistry. The question gives your activated brain a productive direction to move in. The combination works.

CHAPTER 9

When Rejection Feels Like the End of the World

RSD, the stoic view of external judgment, and the difference between caring and collapsing

---

There is a feature of the ADHD experience that almost nobody talks about in public, and almost everybody with ADHD recognizes the moment they hear it described.

It is called rejection sensitive dysphoria. RSD for short.

And if you have it, you already know exactly what it is.

What RSD actually is

Rejection sensitive dysphoria is an intense, often overwhelming emotional response to perceived criticism, rejection, or failure. The key word is perceived. The rejection does not have to be real. A slightly cold tone in an email is enough. A friend who does not reply as quickly as usual. A piece of work that receives less enthusiasm than you hoped for. A meeting where someone seemed distracted.

The response, when it arrives, is not mild disappointment. It is closer to a physical blow. Many people describe it as a sudden drop, as if the floor has disappeared. Others describe it as a wave of shame so intense it temporarily blocks the ability to think clearly.

It typically passes. But while it lasts, it can derail an entire day.

It also, because the response is so disproportionate to most triggers, generates its own secondary layer of shame. Not just the pain of the perceived rejection. But the embarrassment of having reacted so strongly to something that, rationally, was not a big deal.

RSD by the numbers

Research suggests that up to 99 percent of adults with ADHD experience RSD to a clinically significant degree. It is one of the most consistent features of adult ADHD, and one of the least likely to appear in diagnostic criteria or public conversations about the condition.

What the stoics said about external judgment

The stoics spent a great deal of time on the question of how much weight to give to other people's opinions. And their answer was consistently: less than you think, but not zero.

Less than you think, because other people's judgments are not in your control. They depend on the other person's mood, their history, their assumptions, their own fears. Allowing those things to determine your sense of worth is, in stoic terms, outsourcing your stability to something unreliable.

But not zero, because the stoics were also clear that human beings are social creatures, that we need each other, and that the opinions of people we respect and who know us well carry real information worth attending to.

The distinction they drew was between useful feedback and raw judgment. Useful feedback tells you something you can learn from. Raw judgment is just noise about someone else's interior state.

> *"If someone is able to show me that what I think or do is not right, I will happily change, for I seek the truth, by which no one was ever truly harmed."*
> **— Marcus Aurelius, Meditations**

Notice the standard Marcus Aurelius sets. He is open to being wrong. He actively wants to be corrected when he is wrong. But the correction has to show him something. A cold tone, a quick criticism, a perceived slight, those do not show him anything except that the other person had a reaction. That is not the same as evidence.

For people with RSD, this distinction is both useful and, in the moment of the response, almost impossible to apply. The stoic framework does not prevent RSD. But it offers a recovery tool that works, once the first wave has passed.

The two questions that cut through RSD

When the RSD response has arrived and you are in the aftermath, two questions from the stoic tradition are genuinely useful. Not during the spike. After it.

The first question is: is this criticism actually true? Not whether it hurt. Whether it is accurate. Those are different questions, and RSD conflates them constantly. Something can hurt intensely and still be inaccurate. Something can barely sting and still be worth learning from.

The second question is: does this person have the standing to evaluate me on this? Not in a defensive sense. In an honest one. Do they know the full situation? Do they have relevant expertise? Are they someone whose judgment you would trust on a good day?

If the answer to both questions is no, then what you have is not useful information. You have someone's reaction. And someone's reaction, however painful it is to receive, is not a verdict on your worth.

The harder part: when the criticism is partially true

RSD becomes most complicated when the criticism lands on something real.

You did forget the thing. The work was not your best. You were late again. The reaction from the other person was not entirely unwarranted.

In these situations, the RSD response tends to take a partial truth and expand it into a total verdict. A mistake becomes evidence of fundamental failure. A lapse becomes proof of permanent inadequacy. The error was real, but the conclusion the RSD attaches to it is not.

The stoic move here is precise: acknowledge what is true, without accepting what is not.

Yes, I was late. That is accurate. No, that does not mean I am a person who cannot be relied on. Those are two different claims, and only one of them is supported by the evidence.

That is not defensiveness. That is accuracy. And accuracy is where self-respect that actually holds up gets built.

The stoic correction

Take what is useful from criticism. Examine it honestly. Learn from it if there is something to learn. Then let the rest go. Not because it does not hurt. Because it is not information you can use.

The anticipatory RSD problem

One of the most debilitating features of RSD is not the response to actual rejection. It is the anticipation of it.

Because the response is so painful, many people with ADHD develop elaborate avoidance systems. They do not send the work in case it is criticized. They do not raise the idea in the meeting. They do not ask for what they need because the possibility of a no feels unsurvivable.

The stoics had a practice for this: the premeditation of adversity, or premeditatio malorum, which we will cover in a later chapter. In brief: you imagine the difficult outcome in advance, examine it clearly, and discover that it is more survivable than you feared.

The fear of rejection, examined honestly, is almost always larger than the rejection itself. The RSD spike from an imagined rejection tends to be proportional to an actual one. But the actual rejection, once it arrives, also passes. The imagined one never does, because you keep re-living it before it even happens.

The stoic practice is to look at the feared outcome directly. Not to eliminate the fear. To reduce the fog around it so you can see its actual size.

This is not about caring less

A final clarification, because it matters.

The stoic approach to RSD is not about becoming someone who does not care what other people think. The stoics cared deeply about their relationships, their community, their impact on the world. Marcus Aurelius wrote beautifully about the people he loved and what he owed them.

What the stoics were working against was the collapse that happens when external approval becomes the foundation of self-worth. Because a foundation built on other people's reactions is, by definition, unstable. It shifts with every mood, every misread message, every quiet moment that your RSD-brain interprets as rejection.

The work is not to stop caring. The work is to build something underneath the caring. Something that holds when the approval is not there.

The stoics called that something virtue. We might call it self-respect that does not depend on outcome. Either way, it is built slowly, with exactly the kind of small daily practices we have been working on throughout this book.

YOUR PRACTICE

2-minute stoic exercises

Practice 9.1: The RSD debrief (after the spike, 2 minutes)

When an RSD response has passed, before you move on, try this brief debrief. It takes two minutes and is best done in writing, even just a few words on your phone.

- What triggered it? Name the specific thing, not the feeling.
- Is the criticism or rejection actually true? Partially true? Mostly untrue?
- What is the one thing I can learn from this, if anything?
- What is the part that is not useful information, that I can let go?

The debrief is not done during the spike. Wait until the intensity has dropped, even just a little. Then use the questions to convert the raw pain into something you can actually work with.

Practice 9.2: The standing question (as needed)

When you receive criticism that triggers a strong response, before you decide what to do with it, ask one question:

> **The standing question**
>
> Does this person know enough about me, my situation, and this specific thing to be giving me useful feedback right now? If yes: listen carefully. If no: acknowledge the feeling, then set the verdict aside.

You are not dismissing people. You are being precise about whose input is actually worth the weight you are giving it. Most

RSD responses give maximum weight to minimum-information sources. This question rebalances that.

Practice 9.3: The survivability check (for anticipatory RSD)

When you are avoiding something because of the fear of a negative reaction, try this. Take thirty seconds and walk through the actual worst case.

- What is the worst realistic outcome if I do this and it goes badly?
- Have I survived things like this before?
- What would I actually do to get through it if it happened?

The goal is not to reassure yourself that everything will be fine. The goal is to discover that the worst case, while unpleasant, is survivable. You have survived rejections before. The RSD made them feel unsurvivable in the moment. You are still here.

That is the evidence the stoics would point to. Not that it will not hurt. That you can bear it. That distinction is everything when you are standing at the edge of something that matters to you, deciding whether to try.

CHAPTER 10

The Critic That Never Rests

Chronic shame, Seneca's inner dialogue, and how to talk to yourself without doing more damage

---

Most people have an internal critic. A voice that notices mistakes, points out inadequacies, and occasionally delivers an unwelcome verdict on how you are doing as a human being.

People with ADHD tend to have that critic, plus twenty years of extra material.

The material comes from a lifetime of being corrected, redirected, overlooked, and misunderstood by people who did not know they were dealing with a neurological difference. Parents who thought you were not trying. Teachers who thought you were careless. Employers who thought you were unreliable. Partners who thought you did not care enough.

None of those people were necessarily unkind. They just had the wrong map. But the verdicts they delivered, repeated enough times, became part of the inner landscape.

And now the critic does not need anyone else to feed it. It runs on its own.

What shame actually does to the ADHD brain

Shame is not just an unpleasant feeling. It has a measurable effect on the neurology that ADHD already strains.

When shame activates, the stress response follows. Cortisol rises. The prefrontal cortex, already working harder than usual in ADHD brains, becomes less effective. Working memory drops. Emotional regulation becomes more difficult. The very functions you need to do better become less available.

Shame, in other words, does not motivate improvement in ADHD brains. It impairs the capacity for it.

This is the central cruelty of the criticism loop: the more harshly you respond to your own failures, the less equipped you become to avoid them next time. The critic thinks it is helping. It is making things worse.

What research confirms

Dr. Kristin Neff's work on self-compassion, and Dr. Russell Barkley's research on ADHD and emotion, converge on the same finding: self-criticism in people with ADHD does not improve performance. Self-compassion, defined as treating your failures with the same honesty and kindness you would offer a good friend, does.

Seneca on talking to yourself

Seneca wrote more directly about the inner dialogue than almost any other stoic. He was fascinated by the quality of conversation people have with themselves, and deeply concerned about how easily that conversation becomes punishing.

In his letters, he described a practice of internal counsel. When you are struggling or have made a mistake, he said, talk to yourself as you would talk to a friend who came to you in the same situation. Not with false comfort. With honest, caring attention.

> *"We are more severe judges of ourselves than of others, which is good; but we sometimes carry this severity to excess, which is not good."*
> — **Seneca, Letters to Lucilius**

That line is worth sitting with. Seneca is not saying be easy on yourself. He is saying there is a difference between honest self-assessment and punishing excess. The first is useful. The second is not.

For people with ADHD, the internal critic has usually crossed well into excess territory long before it notices. The severity has become the default, not the exception.

The stoic work is not to silence the critic. It is to recalibrate it. To restore the distinction between honest feedback, which you can use, and punishing noise, which you cannot.

The friend standard

Here is a practice that sounds almost too simple, and works almost every time it is applied honestly.

When you notice the internal critic running, stop and ask: would I say this to a friend who came to me with this exact situation?

Not a stranger. A friend. Someone you care about, whose wellbeing matters to you, who you know is trying.

If the answer is no, then what you are saying to yourself is not honesty. It is cruelty. And cruelty is not a useful input.

What would you actually say to that friend? You would probably acknowledge the difficulty. You would probably point out what they did manage, alongside what went wrong. You would probably separate the specific mistake from the global verdict about their character. You would probably remind them that one bad day, or one bad week, or one recurring struggle, is not the final word on who they are.

That is not softness. That is accuracy. And your brain, which is already working harder than most, deserves accurate input from itself.

Naming the critic

A technique that many people with ADHD find surprisingly effective is to give the internal critic a name and a character. Not to befriend it. To create some distance from it.

When the critic arrives with a verdict, you can notice it as a thing that has arrived, rather than a truth that has been delivered. It is the character again, with its usual script. Hello. I see you. I am not going to take that as evidence.

This is the same move as chapter six, where we distinguished between the impression and the judgment about the impression. The critic's verdict is an impression. It is not automatically a judgment you have to accept.

The stoics called this stepping back from the impression. In practice, naming the critic creates the distance you need to step back.

> *"First, tell yourself what kind of person you want to be. Then do what you have to do."*

> — Epictetus, Discourses

The person you want to be is probably not someone who runs a punishing internal monologue. Most people, asked directly, want to be someone who can be honest with themselves without being cruel. That is the target. Not perfection. Not constant positivity. Just the quality of conversation you would offer someone you genuinely cared about.

The apology trap

One more pattern worth naming, because it is very common in adults with ADHD who have internalized a lot of criticism.

The apology trap is the tendency to over-apologize, to preemptively explain your failures, to present yourself as a problem before anyone has suggested you are one. It comes from years of expecting criticism, and trying to manage it by getting there first.

The stoics would recognize this as a form of outsourcing your stability. You are trying to control other people's reactions by preemptively lowering their expectations. The problem is that it also lowers yours. And it signals to your own brain that you are, in fact, a problem.

Honest acknowledgment of a mistake is not the same as the apology trap. You can say I was late, I am working on this, without the extended self-flagellation that follows. The former is accountability. The latter is the critic performing for an audience.

Accountability without self-punishment. That is the stoic standard. It is harder than it sounds, and more useful than almost anything else in this chapter.

YOUR PRACTICE
2-minute stoic exercises

Practice 10.1: The friend audit (2 minutes)

At some point today, you will say something to yourself that you would not say to a friend. When you catch it, write it down. Then write what you would actually say to a friend in the same situation.

Example
What you said to yourself: I cannot believe I forgot that again. I am completely useless. What you would say to a friend: That was a frustrating mistake. You have a lot going on. What can you put in place so it does not happen next time?

The second version is not softer. It is more useful. It moves from verdict to action. That is the difference the stoics were pointing at.

Practice 10.2: Name the critic (once, then ongoing)

Give your internal critic a name. Make it slightly absurd. Something that signals: this is a character, not a truth-teller.

Then, when it arrives with a verdict, acknowledge it by name. Out loud or in your head.

There it is again. I hear you. I am not accepting that as evidence today.

You are not arguing with it. You are not suppressing it. You are noticing it, which is the stoic move, and declining to give it automatic authority over your assessment of yourself.

Practice 10.3: The Seneca debrief (2 minutes, end of day)

Seneca's inner counsel practice, adapted for ADHD:

- Name one thing that went wrong today. State it factually, without verdict.
- Name one thing the difficulty was actually about. What executive function, what circumstance, what genuine challenge was involved?
- Name one thing you would do differently. Specific and small.
- Name one thing you did that was worth acknowledging. Just one. Be honest.

Four steps. Two minutes. The structure matters because the ADHD brain left to its own devices tends to either ruminate on step one indefinitely or skip to something else entirely. The structure keeps you moving through all four.

CHAPTER 11

Anger Arrives Fast

Seneca on rage, the ADHD anger response, and what you are actually defending

---

Seneca wrote an entire treatise on anger. Three books. It is the longest piece of writing he left us on any single subject.

That tells you something about how seriously he took it.

He opens the first book with a description of what anger looks like from the outside: the red face, the shaking hands, the voice that changes register, the eyes that go somewhere else. He is clinical about it, almost unnervingly so. And then he says something that most people in the ancient world, and many people today, would find surprising.

He says anger is always a choice. Not a feeling that happens to you. A judgment you make, often in a fraction of a second, but a judgment nonetheless.

If you have ADHD, your first response to that claim might be something between skepticism and outrage. Because the experience of anger in ADHD does not feel like a choice. It feels like a weather event. It arrives without warning, at full intensity, before you have had any chance to evaluate anything.

Seneca knew this. He did not say anger is easy to intercept. He said it is, in principle, always preceded by a judgment. And that judgment, even a very fast one, is where the work lives.

Why ADHD anger is different in intensity, not in kind

The anger response in ADHD is not a different animal from anger in general. It is the same animal running faster, hitting harder, and leaving faster.

The neurological reasons are now well understood. The same dopamine and norepinephrine dysregulation that affects attention and working memory also affects the speed and intensity of emotional responses. The amygdala fires earlier. The prefrontal brake arrives later. The gap between stimulus and full emotional activation is shorter than in neurotypical brains.

This means two things that are worth holding at the same time.

First: the intensity of the anger is not evidence of its validity. A response can be disproportionately strong without the underlying grievance being wrong. You might be entirely right that something unfair has happened. The anger's amplitude does not prove or disprove that.

Second: the speed of arrival does not eliminate the possibility of a pause. The pause is smaller. It requires more practice to access. But it exists. And practicing it, as Seneca insisted, makes it larger over time.

What Seneca got right

Seneca argued that the first moment of anger, the initial heat, is largely involuntary. What we do with that heat is not. The practice is not to prevent the heat. It is to lengthen the time between the heat and the action.

What the anger is actually defending

Here is the stoic question about anger that most people never reach, because they are too busy managing the response: what value is the anger defending?

Anger is almost always a signal that something you care about has been violated. Fairness. Respect. Your time. Someone else's wellbeing. Your sense of competence. Your autonomy. The anger is the alarm system for your values.

This is important for two reasons.

The first is that it means anger is not irrational by nature. If someone has genuinely violated something you reasonably care about, the anger is an accurate signal. The problem is not the signal. The problem is what you do in response to it.

The second is that understanding what the anger is defending gives you a much more precise target for action. Instead of responding to the full emotional charge, you can ask: what specifically has been violated here, and what is the most effective way to address that?

That shift from reacting to the feeling to responding to the value underneath it is one of the most practically useful moves in the entire stoic toolkit. And for ADHD brains, where the feeling tends to dominate the room, having a question that redirects attention to the value underneath is genuinely helpful.

> *"Consider how much more you often suffer from your anger and grief than from those very things for which you are angry and grieved."*
> **— Marcus Aurelius, Meditations**

This is one of Marcus Aurelius's most direct observations, and it lands differently depending on where you are in the anger cycle. In the middle of the spike, it feels irrelevant. In the aftermath, it is often painfully accurate.

The suffering that follows an angry response, the regret, the damage to relationships, the energy cost, is frequently larger than the original grievance that triggered it. Not always. But often enough to be worth tracking.

The ADHD aftermath

One of the distinctive features of ADHD anger is the aftermath.

In many people with ADHD, the anger arrives fast, peaks quickly, and then dissipates in a way that feels, from the inside, almost complete. The event is over. The anger has passed.

But for the people on the receiving end, the event is not over. They are still processing what happened. They may still be hurt, or frightened, or confused. The asymmetry between how quickly the person with ADHD has moved on and how long the impact lingers for others is one of the most common sources of relationship difficulty in adult ADHD.

Understanding this asymmetry does not undo it. But it changes the conversation you can have about it. And it changes the kind of repair you know to offer.

Repair as a stoic practice

The stoics were not sentimentalists, but they were clear about the obligations that come with living among other people. When you have caused harm, you attend to it. Not through extended self-punishment, but through honest acknowledgment and practical repair.

For ADHD, where angry responses happen more frequently and often more intensely than intended, repair is not optional. It is a core skill.

And repair, done well, is not the same as excessive apology. It is specific, honest, and forward-looking. It says: what happened, why it happened, what I am working on, and what I will do differently. It does not say: I am a terrible person and you should not trust me.

The first version rebuilds the relationship. The second version makes the other person manage your shame as well as their own experience. That is not repair. That is transferring the weight.

The stoic repair formula

Name what happened factually. Acknowledge the impact on the other person. State one specific thing you are working on. Ask what they need. Then stop talking.

Anger and self-knowledge

Seneca's final word on anger, in the third book of his treatise, is perhaps the most useful one for people with ADHD.

He says: study your anger. Learn its patterns. Know what triggers it, what makes it worse, what makes it shorter. Not to eliminate it. To understand it well enough that it stops surprising you.

For a brain where anger arrives fast and without much warning, that kind of self-knowledge is protective. Not because it prevents every spike. Because it means you know the terrain. You know which situations are higher risk. You know what your anger tends to be defending. You know what the aftermath usually looks like and what repair you will need to do.

That is not the same as control. But it is something more sustainable than control. It is understanding. And understanding your own anger is the beginning of working with it rather than being worked by it.

YOUR PRACTICE
2-minute stoic exercises

Practice 11.1: Map the pattern (this week)

This week, after any moment of significant anger, spend two minutes mapping it. Not in the middle of the spike. After.

- What triggered it? Be specific about the actual event.
- What value was being violated? What were you actually defending?
- What did you do with the anger? What was the consequence?
- What would you do differently with that information next time?

Do this for five days and you will have a map of your anger patterns that is more useful than anything a therapist could hand you, because it is yours and it is accurate.

Practice 11.2: The value question (in the moment, 10 seconds)

When you notice anger arriving, before saying or doing anything, try one internal question:

> **The value question**
>
> What is this anger defending right now? Fairness? Respect? My time? Someone I care about? Name the value, not the feeling. The value points to the response. The feeling alone does not.

You will not always manage this in the moment. That is fine. Practice it after the fact first, until it becomes more available in real time. That is how all stoic practice works: rehearsal creates availability.

Practice 11.3: The repair protocol (as needed)

After an angry response that caused damage, use the four-part repair:

- Name what happened: I raised my voice when you were late. That was not okay.
- Acknowledge the impact: I imagine that felt frightening or disrespectful.
- State what you are working on: I am practicing pausing before I react to this kind of trigger.
- Ask what they need: What would help you right now?

Then stop. Do not add self-flagellation. Do not ask them to reassure you. The repair is for them, not for your relief. Keep those two things separate and the repair will actually work.

CHAPTER 12

Time Is the Strangest Thing

ADHD time blindness, memento mori, and making the future feel real enough to care about

---

Ask someone without ADHD what they are doing in three weeks, and they will probably give you a reasonable answer. They have some mental map of the coming weeks. They can feel the distance between now and then in a way that informs their decisions.

Ask someone with ADHD the same question, and you are likely to get one of two responses. Either a very vague answer because three weeks is so far away it barely registers as real, or a very specific answer because they have externalized the information into a calendar and are reading it back to you, rather than actually sensing the time.

This is not a memory problem. It is a time perception problem. And it is one of the most underappreciated features of the ADHD experience.

The two-mode time system

Dr. Russell Barkley, whose work on ADHD executive functions is among the most cited in the field, describes the ADHD experience of time as essentially binary.

There is now. And there is not now.

Things that are happening right now are vivid, real, and motivating. Things that are not happening right now, whether they are in the future or the recent past, tend to fade into a kind of undifferentiated not-now. A deadline three weeks away and a deadline three months away feel roughly equally unreal until the moment they become now.

This is why the last-minute crisis is such a consistent feature of ADHD life. Not laziness. Not poor planning. The future, until it becomes the present, simply does not exert the same pull on the ADHD brain that it does on neurotypical ones.

The technical term

Time blindness is the informal term for deficits in prospective memory and temporal self-monitoring. The ADHD brain has reduced activation in the regions responsible for mentally projecting yourself into the future, which makes future consequences less real, and therefore less motivating, than present experience.

What the stoics understood about time

The stoics were obsessed with time. Not with productivity or scheduling, but with the nature of time itself and what it means for how we live.

Their central observation was that most people live as though they have unlimited time. They defer important things. They treat the present as a waiting room for some future moment when life will really begin. And then, without realizing it, they run out of future.

Seneca wrote an entire essay about this, On the Shortness of Life, and it remains one of the most direct pieces of writing in the philosophical tradition. He is not gentle about it.

> *"It is not that we have a short time to live, but that we waste a great deal of it. Life is long enough, and a sufficiently generous amount has been given to us for the highest achievements if it were all well invested."*
> — **Seneca, On the Shortness of Life**

What Seneca is diagnosing sounds, at first, like the opposite of the ADHD problem. He is criticizing people who defer life. ADHD people tend to be intensely present. They do not defer. They live almost entirely in now.

But look more carefully. The underlying problem is the same: an inability to hold past, present, and future in meaningful relationship to each other. Seneca's contemporaries lived as if the future were infinite. People with ADHD live as if the future barely exists. Different presentations of the same failure to inhabit time fully.

Memento mori: the future that actually works

The stoics developed a practice called memento mori. Remember that you will die.

Before you put the book down, stay with this for a moment. Because this is not the morbid exercise it sounds like. In practice, it is the opposite.

The stoics used the awareness of mortality not to generate fear or despair, but to make the present feel vivid and the near future feel real. When you genuinely hold the finite nature of your time, the things that matter become clearer, and the things that do not become easier to let go of.

For ADHD brains, where the future is chronically underrepresented in motivation, memento mori does something specific and useful: it makes the future arrive emotionally, without requiring it to arrive temporally.

In other words: you cannot always feel the reality of a deadline three weeks away. But you can sometimes feel the reality of your finite time. And that feeling, once accessed, does what deadlines are supposed to do. It makes now feel connected to something that matters.

Making the future feel real: practical strategies

The stoic insight and the neuroscience of ADHD time blindness point toward the same set of practical approaches.

The future needs to be made concrete and sensory. Not abstract. Not a date on a calendar. Something you can see, hear, or feel.

This is why some of the most effective ADHD time management strategies involve making future states physically present. A visual countdown. A photo of the place you will be in three weeks. A voice memo from your past self to your future self. Objects that represent future commitments placed where you will encounter them now.

The stoics did a version of this with their premeditation practices. They would vividly imagine future scenarios, in detail, to bring them into emotional present-tense. The technique was philosophical, but the mechanism is the same: specificity and sensory detail create emotional reality that abstract planning cannot.

> *"Let us prepare our minds as if we had come to the very end of life. Let us postpone nothing. Let us balance life's books each day."*
> — **Seneca, Letters to Lucilius**

Balance life's books each day. For ADHD, this is not a metaphor about organization. It is an instruction about closing loops. Ending each day with some sense of what happened, what matters, and what tomorrow holds. Not as a productivity exercise. As a practice of making time feel real.

Urgency without crisis

One of the gifts, if you can call it that, of ADHD time blindness is that when the future finally becomes now, the focus that arrives is often extraordinary.

The last-minute crisis mode that ADHD brains slip into is not ideal. But it reveals something important: the capacity for intense engagement is there. The problem is that it only activates reliably under conditions of genuine urgency.

The stoic and neuroscientific goal is not to eliminate that capacity. It is to learn to create conditions that activate it without requiring an actual crisis. Artificial deadlines. Stakes that are real enough to matter. Accountability to someone whose opinion you care about. A clear picture of why this particular thing matters in the context of the finite time you actually have.

These are not tricks. They are ways of giving the ADHD brain what it needs to engage with the future before the future is already burning.

YOUR PRACTICE
2-minute stoic exercises

Practice 12.1: The mortality minute (once, seriously)

This practice asks something of you, so read it before deciding whether to do it.

Find five minutes alone. No phone. Then answer this question in writing, as specifically and honestly as you can:

The question
If I had one year left, what would I stop spending time on? What would I start? What would I make sure happened?

This is not a bucket list exercise. It is a values clarification. The answers tend to be surprisingly specific, and surprisingly consistent with what you already know matters to you. The mortality frame just strips away the comfortable deferral.

Read what you wrote. Then ask: what is one thing from this list I could start or stop this week?

Practice 12.2: Make the future concrete (5 minutes, once a week)

Pick one thing coming up in the next two to four weeks that matters to you. Then spend five minutes making it sensory and specific.

- Write three sentences about what it will look, sound, or feel like when it happens.
- Write one sentence about why it matters to you specifically.
- Write one thing you will do today that moves toward it.

You are not planning. You are making the future real enough to feel. The third step is the one that actually bridges the two-mode time system, because it creates a now action connected to a not-now outcome.

Practice 12.3: The daily close (2 minutes, end of day)

Seneca's balance the books practice, adapted for ADHD:

1. One thing that happened today that mattered.
2. One thing left undone that needs to move to tomorrow.
3. One thing about tomorrow I am holding in my mind.

Three bullets. Two minutes. The goal is not comprehensive review. It is continuity. Giving the ADHD brain a thread that runs from today into tomorrow, instead of the clean break that makes each morning feel like starting from zero.

Seneca wrote that we should treat each day as a small life. Complete in itself, but connected to what comes before and after. For a brain that lives mostly in now, building that thread is not optional. It is the practice.

CHAPTER 13

Loving How You Function

Amor fati, radical acceptance, and building a life that fits your actual brain

---

There is a Latin phrase that Nietzsche borrowed from the stoics and made famous, though the stoics themselves had been living it for centuries before he arrived.

Amor fati. Love of fate.

Not tolerance of fate. Not grudging acceptance of fate. Love of it.

If you have ADHD, your first reaction to that phrase might be something between confusion and mild irritation. Love of the thing that made school feel like a trap, that cost you jobs, that damaged relationships, that left you feeling for years like you were fundamentally failing at being a person?

That seems like a lot to ask.

So let us be precise about what amor fati actually means, because it is not what it sounds like from the outside.

What amor fati is not

Amor fati is not pretending that everything is fine. It is not a spiritual bypass that insists your difficulties are not real. It is not the toxic positivity of finding a silver lining in every setback.

Marcus Aurelius, who lived the philosophy as seriously as anyone, did not love the death of his children. He did not love the wars he was forced to fight. He did not love the political betrayals he endured. He grieved. He suffered. He wrote about it.

What he practiced was something more specific and more demanding: accepting reality as the starting point for everything else. Not fighting the fact of what had happened. Working from what was actually true rather than from what he wished were true.

> *"Accept the things to which fate binds you, and love the people with whom fate brings you together, and do so with all your heart."*
> **— Marcus Aurelius, Meditations**

Accept and love are doing different work in that sentence. Accept applies to circumstances. Love applies to people. The stoic is not being asked to love every difficulty. They are being asked to stop fighting the reality of it, and to bring genuine care to the human relationships inside it.

For ADHD, this distinction is everything.

The exhaustion of fighting your own brain

One of the most common experiences of adults with ADHD, particularly those diagnosed late, is the exhaustion of having spent years trying to be a different kind of person.

Not just trying harder. Trying to be neurologically different. Trying to sustain attention the way neurotypical people do. Trying to maintain systems that were designed for a different kind of mind.

Trying to meet expectations built on assumptions that were never true for you.

That effort is enormous. And it is largely wasted, not because the trying does not matter, but because it is aimed at the wrong target. You cannot change your neurology through willpower. You can change how you work with it.

That shift, from fighting your brain to working with it, is what amor fati looks like in practice for people with ADHD. It is not giving up. It is redirecting enormous amounts of energy toward strategies that actually fit the brain you have.

The reframe

Acceptance is not the opposite of effort. It is the precondition for effort that works. You cannot build an effective life on a false picture of who you are. Amor fati starts with getting the picture right.

What your brain actually needs

The stoic practice of self-knowledge, which we have been building throughout this book, leads here: to a clear picture of what conditions your brain actually needs to function well, as opposed to what conditions you have been told you should be able to function in.

People with ADHD tend to do significantly better under specific conditions, and significantly worse under others. Not because of weakness. Because of neurology.

Better under conditions of: novelty, genuine interest, clear and meaningful purpose, appropriate stimulation, flexibility in timing and environment, accountability to someone they care about, and visible progress.

Worse under conditions of: repetitive low-stimulation tasks, ambiguous goals, long time horizons with no intermediate checkpoints, isolation, and environments with no control over sensory input.

Most conventional work and life structures are built around the second list. That is not a personal failing. It is a mismatch between an environment and a brain.

Amor fati, applied practically, means designing your life to maximize the first list and minimize the second, to the extent that is within your control. Not perfectly. Not all at once. But deliberately, and without apologizing for the fact that you need different conditions than the person next to you.

The ADHD strengths that amor fati reveals

There is something else that becomes visible when you stop fighting your brain and start working with it.

The same features that create problems in conventional environments also produce things that are genuinely valuable, and not just in a compensatory way. Not the consolation prize of creativity in exchange for the inability to file taxes on time.

The ADHD brain's hunger for novelty drives genuine innovation. Its tendency to make unexpected connections produces ideas that linear thinking misses. Its intensity of engagement, when it lands on the right thing, produces work of a quality that sustained moderate effort rarely achieves. Its sensitivity to injustice and its empathy for people who are struggling come from the same emotional attunement that makes regulation difficult.

These are not spins on a bad situation. They are real. And amor fati is partly the practice of holding all of it together, the genuine difficulties and the genuine strengths, and building a life that makes honest use of both.

> *"Waste no more time arguing about what a good man should be. Be one."*
> — **Marcus Aurelius, Meditations**

The arguing, in this context, is the endless internal negotiation about what kind of brain you should have. The being is what happens when you take the brain you have and build the best possible life from it.

That is the whole instruction. It is simple in theory and requires everything in practice.

Acceptance is not a destination

A final note, because this comes up often.

Amor fati is not a state you arrive at and maintain forever. It is a practice you return to. There will be days when the ADHD difficulties are hard enough that acceptance feels impossible. There will be moments when you are genuinely grieving the life you might have had with a different neurological profile.

That grief is valid. The stoics did not deny grief. They just did not let it become the permanent operating condition.

The practice is to return. To notice when you are back in the fight against your own brain, and to come back to the work of building from what is actually there. Not because what is there is always enough. Because it is what you have to work with, and working with it honestly is the only path to a life that is actually yours.

YOUR PRACTICE
2-minute stoic exercises

Practice 13.1: The conditions audit (2 minutes)

Write two lists as honestly as you can.

Conditions where my brain works well:

Think of specific times when you were genuinely productive, engaged, or effective. What was present? What was absent?

Conditions where my brain consistently struggles:

Think of recurring situations that reliably drain or block you. What do they have in common?

Then ask: of the things on the second list, which ones are actually changeable? What is one adjustment you could make this week to shift the conditions even slightly?

Practice 13.2: The amor fati reframe (as needed)

When you notice yourself in a fight against your own brain, try this single question:

Ask yourself
What would it look like to work with this, rather than against it? Not to fix it. Not to overcome it. To build something that fits it.

The answer is not always available immediately. But the question itself shifts the direction of the effort. From resistance to design. That shift is amor fati in practice.

Practice 13.3: The honest strengths inventory (once)

Write down three things you do genuinely well that are connected to how your brain works. Not things you wish you were good at. Things you actually are.

Be specific. Not creative, but notices patterns others miss. Not empathetic, but knows when someone in the room is not okay before they say anything.

Then ask: am I building a life that uses these? If not, what is one place where I could?

This is not positive thinking. It is accurate inventory. Amor fati requires both sides of the ledger.

CHAPTER 14

Planning for Failure

Premeditatio malorum, negative visualization, and why imagining the worst is the most practical thing you can do

---

There is a stoic practice that sounds, on first hearing, like the last thing someone with an anxious or hyperactive mind should do.

It is called premeditatio malorum. The premeditation of adversity. Before something important happens, you deliberately imagine what could go wrong.

Specifically. Vividly. In detail.

If your instinct is that this would make things worse, not better, you are in good company. Most people have that instinct. And most people are wrong about it, for reasons that turn out to be deeply relevant to the ADHD experience.

Why the stoics practiced negative visualization

The stoics were not pessimists. They were realists who noticed something important: most human suffering does not come from bad things happening. It comes from the gap between what we expected and what actually occurred.

When you have mentally rehearsed a difficulty in advance, it arrives with less shock. You have already thought about how you would respond. You have already identified the resources you would need. The surprise element, which is often what turns a manageable problem into a crisis, has been reduced.

This is not the same as worrying. Worry is passive and repetitive. It circles the feared outcome without ever examining it clearly. Premeditatio malorum is active and structured. You look directly at the possible failure, think through what you would actually do, and then move on.

> *"Let us prepare our minds as if we had come to the very end of life. Let us postpone nothing."*
> **— Seneca, Letters to Lucilius**

Seneca is not suggesting you live in dread. He is suggesting that the person who has mentally prepared for difficulty is more free, not less, because they are not spending energy on the unconscious avoidance of thinking about what might go wrong.

Why this is particularly useful for ADHD

For ADHD brains, premeditatio malorum addresses two specific problems that conventional planning does not.

The first is the planning fallacy. People with ADHD tend to underestimate how long things will take, how many things can go wrong, and how much energy tasks will actually require. This is not because they are bad at planning in theory. It is because planning requires projecting the self into the future, and as we discussed in chapter twelve, ADHD brains do this less reliably than neurotypical ones.

Negative visualization forces that future projection. By deliberately imagining what could go wrong, you are doing the exact cognitive work that ADHD tends to skip: making the future real enough to plan for.

The second problem is the fear of failure that produces avoidance. Many people with ADHD avoid starting things partly because the possible failure feels unsurvivable, and better not to try than to find out. Premeditatio malorum, done carefully, reveals that the feared outcome is almost always more survivable than the avoidance assumes.

The key distinction

Premeditatio malorum is not catastrophizing. Catastrophizing spirals: the bad thing happens, then worse things follow, then everything collapses. Premeditatio malorum is bounded: what is the realistic worst case, and what would I actually do? The second question is what catastrophizing never reaches.

The practical structure

Effective negative visualization has a structure. Without it, the practice does tip into anxiety. With it, it is genuinely useful.

The structure has three steps.

Step one: identify the specific feared outcome. Not a vague sense that things might go badly. The specific thing. I will be late and it will make a bad impression. I will start and not finish and feel ashamed. The work will be rejected and I will spiral.

Step two: examine it honestly. How likely is this, really? What would actually happen if it did? Have I survived things like this before? What resources would I have available?

Step three: decide what you would do if it happened. Not how you would feel. What you would do. This is the step that converts the feared outcome from a vague dread into a manageable scenario.

After step three, you move on. The practice is complete. You have looked at the thing, understood it, prepared for it, and now you act anyway.

Applied to ADHD-specific failures

The most valuable application of this practice for people with ADHD is around the failures that tend to recur. Not random setbacks, but the patterns.

You start projects and do not finish them. You forget important things despite good intentions. You commit to more than you can sustain. You lose focus at critical moments. You react too strongly and damage something you wanted to protect.

These are not mysteries. You know they happen. Premeditatio malorum applied to your own patterns sounds like this: I know that around week three of a new project, my interest typically drops and I risk abandoning it. What will I do when that happens?

Not if. When. The stoic planning assumes the difficulty is coming, because experience tells you it is. The question is only what you will do when it arrives.

That shift from surprise to preparation changes the entire texture of the experience when it comes. You are not failing again. You are encountering the thing you already planned for.

> *"Rehearse them in your mind: exile, torture, war, shipwreck. All the terms of our human lot should be before our eyes."*
> **— Seneca, Letters to Lucilius**

Seneca's list is dramatic. Yours can be more mundane. The forgetting. The late start. The abandoned system. The overcommitment. These are the shipwrecks of the ADHD life, and they are worth rehearsing in exactly the way Seneca describes.

The relief on the other side

Here is something that surprises most people the first time they do this practice properly.

After you have clearly imagined the worst realistic outcome and thought through what you would actually do, the anxiety about it decreases. Not because the outcome has become less possible. Because you have stopped running from the thought of it.

The anxiety was being fed by avoidance. Every time you pushed the feared thought away, it came back larger. Premeditatio malorum works partly because it reverses that process. You turn toward the thing. You look at it. You discover it has edges. And things with edges are manageable in a way that formless dread is not.

For an ADHD brain that tends to experience difficulty as an undifferentiated overwhelm, finding the edges of a feared outcome is not a small thing. It is the difference between paralysis and preparation.

YOUR PRACTICE
2-minute stoic exercises

Practice 14.1: The three-step premeditation (2 minutes, before anything important)

Before a task, event, or commitment that you are avoiding or anxious about, run the three steps:

- What specifically am I afraid will go wrong?
- How likely is it? Have I survived this before? What would actually happen?
- What would I do if it happened? Specifically. One action.

Write the answers, even briefly. The writing matters because the ADHD brain will skip step three if left to its own devices. Step three is where the practice becomes useful.

Practice 14.2: The pattern premeditation (once a month)

Pick one recurring ADHD pattern that tends to cause problems. The one you most wish you handled differently.

Then write: when this happens next, which it will, here is exactly what I will do.

> **Example**
>
> Pattern: I commit to things I cannot sustain and then disappear when I cannot deliver. Premeditation: When I feel the pull to say yes to something I am not sure I can do, I will say I need to check my capacity and come back to you tomorrow. That is my one move.

One move. Specific. Written down. That is enough. You are not redesigning your character. You are installing one prepared response for one recurring situation.

Practice 14.3: The survivability test (as needed)

When you are avoiding something because the feared outcome feels unsurvivable, ask these three questions in writing:

- What is the worst realistic outcome, not the catastrophic fantasy, the realistic one?
- Have I survived something comparable before?
- What is one thing I would do on the other side of it?

The third question is the one that breaks the avoidance. Because once you can see yourself on the other side of the feared outcome doing something, it is no longer the end of everything. It is an event in a life that continues.

That is not reassurance. That is accuracy. And accuracy is what the stoics were always after.

CHAPTER 15

Fewer Decisions, More Clarity

Stoic virtue, decision fatigue, and why knowing what you stand for is the most practical thing you can do

---

Every decision you make costs something. Not money. Energy. The cognitive resource that psychologists call decision-making capacity, and that depletes across a day the way a battery depletes under load.

This matters for everyone. It matters more for people with ADHD.

Because the ADHD brain is already running more cognitive load than average, managing attention, inhibiting impulses, regulating emotions, tracking time, holding working memory, all of it simultaneously and with less neurological efficiency than neurotypical brains. Adding a high volume of daily decisions to that load is not a neutral act. It accelerates the depletion.

The result is familiar: by mid-afternoon, or sometimes earlier, the capacity for good decisions has dropped noticeably. You say yes to things you should decline. You choose the easy option over the right one. You react instead of respond. You do the urgent thing instead of the important one.

This is not weakness. It is exhausted cognitive infrastructure.

What the stoics discovered about values and decisions

The stoics arrived at a solution to this problem not through neuroscience, which did not exist, but through careful observation of how good people actually live.

Their observation was this: people who live well do not make most of their decisions fresh. They have already decided, at a deep level, what kind of person they want to be and what they stand for. And when a situation arises, they do not have to reason from scratch. They consult the decision that was already made.

This is what the stoics meant by virtue. Not a set of moral rules to follow. A settled orientation toward what matters, from which individual decisions flow naturally.

> *"If you know what you are, the right actions follow. If you do not know what you are, every situation is a new problem."*
> **— Epictetus, Discourses**

For people with ADHD, where decision fatigue arrives faster and hits harder, this insight is not abstract philosophy. It is a practical cognitive strategy. The fewer novel decisions your brain has to generate from scratch, the more capacity it retains for the things that genuinely require fresh thinking.

The four stoic virtues, translated

The stoics organized their values around four cardinal virtues. The language is old, but the content is relevant.

Wisdom: knowing what is actually true and what actually matters, rather than what feels urgent or what other people say is important. For ADHD, this is the capacity to distinguish between the genuinely important and the merely stimulating.

Courage: doing what you know is right even when it is uncomfortable, including being honest about your limitations, asking for what you need, and trying again after failure.

Justice: treating other people fairly and taking seriously your impact on the people around you, including the impact of ADHD behaviors on those who live and work with you.

Temperance: not excess, but proportion. Matching your response to the actual size of the situation. Neither too much nor too little. For ADHD, this is one of the most relevant virtues and one of the hardest.

A useful exercise

Take each virtue and ask: what would this look like in one specific recurring situation in my life? Not in general. In a specific situation. The more concrete the virtue becomes, the more available it is when you need it.

Pre-deciding as an ADHD strategy

The practical application of stoic virtue for ADHD is what some psychologists call pre-deciding: making certain decisions in advance, when your cognitive resources are high, so you do not have to make them again under load.

This is not a new idea. The stoics practiced it as a matter of course. Marcus Aurelius wrote about knowing in advance how he intended to respond to common provocations. Epictetus taught his students to decide before they entered difficult situations what their values required of them.

For ADHD, pre-deciding covers a surprisingly wide range of daily life. It covers things like: I do not check email before 9am. I do not agree to new commitments on the same day they are proposed. When I am overwhelmed, my first move is always to write down what is in my head before I try to act on any of it.

None of these are rules imposed from outside. They are decisions made in advance by someone who knows their own patterns and has chosen, deliberately, how to respond to them. That is stoic virtue made operational.

The ADHD tax and what to do about it

There is a concept in the ADHD community called the ADHD tax: the extra time, money, energy, and opportunity that the condition costs. Late fees from forgotten bills. Relationships strained by reactive behavior. Careers limited by executive function challenges. The cumulative weight of a brain that requires more management than most.

The stoic response to the ADHD tax is not to pretend it does not exist. It does. It is to build the kind of values-based structure that reduces the decisions made under depletion, which is where most of the tax gets levied.

Most of the costly mistakes in ADHD life, the impulsive spending, the careless words, the abandoned commitments, happen not because the person does not know better, but because they made the decision when their cognitive resources were already exhausted. The stoic strategy is to pre-decide as much as possible, so that the depleted brain has fewer original decisions to make and more pre-settled ground to stand on.

> *"First say to yourself what you would be; and then do what you have to do."*
> — **Epictetus, Discourses**

What you would be. Not what you should do in this situation. What kind of person you are. That knowledge comes first. And for people with ADHD, where the situation itself can be overwhelming enough to crowd out everything else, having that knowledge already settled is not a luxury. It is a functional necessity.

Small values, daily decisions

The stoic virtues sound large. Wisdom. Courage. Justice. Temperance. They sound like the qualities of senators and philosophers.

In practice, they operate at the scale of ordinary days. The courage to tell someone you need more time. The wisdom to recognize that the interesting new project is not actually the most important one right now. The justice of following through on a commitment even when the excitement has faded. The temperance of stopping at enough instead of continuing until you crash.

Those are not grand acts. They are small daily moves. And they compound.

Over a week of small stoic decisions, you start to notice that your energy is being spent differently. Not because you have more of it. Because you are wasting less of it on decisions that were already made.

YOUR PRACTICE
2-minute stoic exercises

Practice 15.1: Your three non-negotiables (2 minutes, once)

Write down three personal rules that you will follow regardless of how depleted you feel. These should be pre-decided responses to your most common costly mistakes.

They should follow this format: when X happens, I always do Y.

Examples
When I am asked to commit to something new, I always wait 24 hours before saying yes. When I feel overwhelmed, I always write down what is in my head before I do anything else. When I have an angry impulse in a message or email, I always wait one hour before sending.

Three rules. Written down. Somewhere you will see them. These are your pre-decisions. They are not rules someone else made for you. They are decisions you made for yourself, in advance, when you were thinking clearly.

Practice 15.2: The virtue checkpoint (2 minutes, weekly)

Once a week, pick one of the four stoic virtues and ask how it showed up in your week.

- Wisdom: did I distinguish between what felt urgent and what actually mattered?
- Courage: did I do the thing I knew was right when it was uncomfortable?
- Justice: did I take seriously my impact on the people around me?
- Temperance: did I match my response to the actual size of the situation?

One virtue per week. Not all four at once. You are building a practice, not completing a checklist.

Practice 15.3: Decision triage (as needed)

When you are facing multiple decisions and feeling depleted, run a quick triage before engaging with any of them:

- Which of these have I already pre-decided? Apply the rule and move on.
- Which of these genuinely need fresh thinking? These get my attention now.
- Which of these can wait until I have more capacity? Schedule them and stop thinking about them.

Most people with ADHD treat all decisions as equally urgent and equally novel. The triage reveals that most are not. That clarity alone reduces the cognitive load considerably.

The stoics called this distinguishing between what is up to you and what is not. The triage is the same move, applied to your daily decision stack.

CHAPTER 16

The Environment Is the Strategy

Epictetus on what is yours to control, and why designing your surroundings is the most stoic thing you can do

---

Epictetus began with almost nothing.

He was born into slavery, suffered a physical injury that left him with a permanent disability, and spent the first years of his life with no control over where he went, what he did, or who he was allowed to be.

And from that position, he built one of the most influential philosophies of self-determination in human history.

The lesson he drew from his own circumstances was not that the external world does not matter. It clearly does. The lesson was more precise: you cannot always control what the world does, but you can almost always control how you arrange your relationship to it.

For people with ADHD, that insight has a very practical application. You cannot change your neurology. But you can change your environment. And changing your environment is, in many cases, more effective than trying to change your behavior directly.

Why environment matters more for ADHD brains

Neurotypical brains have more reliable access to top-down control. They can, with effort and intention, override environmental distractions, sustain attention through low-stimulation periods, and initiate tasks even when conditions are not ideal.

ADHD brains rely more heavily on bottom-up activation. The environment itself has to do more of the work. A well-designed environment can make the right behavior significantly easier. A poorly designed one makes it nearly impossible, regardless of how much the person wants to do better.

This is not an excuse for avoiding effort. It is a description of how the ADHD brain actually works, and designing around it is not cheating. It is working with the nature you have. Which, as we have established, is the entire stoic project.

The key insight

For neurotypical brains, willpower is the primary tool and environment is the backup. For ADHD brains, environment is the primary tool and willpower is what you use when environment fails. Reversing this priority changes everything.

What Epictetus would say about your desk

Epictetus divided the world into things that are up to us and things that are not. But he was also clear that within the category of things that are up to us, we have significant latitude, and we should use it deliberately.

Your physical environment is, to a meaningful degree, up to you. Not entirely. You do not always choose your workplace or your home. But within whatever space you inhabit, there is almost always more room for intentional design than most people use.

What is on your desk? What is visible when you sit down to work? What sounds reach you? What temperature are you at? How much of what you can see is related to what you are trying to do, and how much of it is competing for your attention?

These are not trivial questions for an ADHD brain. They are the difference between a morning that flows and a morning that does not.

> *"Make the best use of what is in your power, and take the rest as it happens."*
> — **Epictetus, Enchiridion**

Making the best use of what is in your power includes making the best use of your power to shape the space around you. That is not a minor thing. For many people with ADHD, it is the highest-leverage intervention available.

Friction as a design tool

Behavioral psychology has a concept called friction: the ease or difficulty of performing a behavior. High friction means there are obstacles in the way. Low friction means the path is clear.

For ADHD, managing friction is one of the most powerful environmental strategies available. Not through willpower, but through design.

You want to reduce friction for behaviors that serve you. Put the book you want to read on your pillow. Put the vitamins next to the coffee maker. Put the running shoes by the door. Make the right thing the easy thing, because when your initiation system is unreliable, the easy thing is the thing that happens.

You want to increase friction for behaviors that do not serve you. Put your phone in another room when you need to focus. Log out of social media so opening it requires an extra step. Create distance between yourself and the impulse. The ADHD brain will often abandon an impulse if the path to it is slightly longer, because the impulse fades faster than the friction.

This is not a trick. It is engineering. You are designing the conditions under which your brain operates, rather than hoping your brain will overcome the conditions through effort alone.

The stoic home and workspace

Marcus Aurelius was known for the deliberate simplicity of his personal spaces. He was emperor of Rome and could have surrounded himself with anything. He chose environments that supported reflection and focus rather than stimulation and display.

That was not asceticism for its own sake. It was design. He knew that his best thinking required certain conditions, and he created those conditions rather than hoping they would appear.

For people with ADHD, the equivalent practice is personal and specific. What your brain needs is not the same as what anyone else's brain needs. Some ADHD brains do their best work in coffee shops with background noise. Others need complete silence. Some need visual order to think. Others work better in what looks like chaos to everyone else but has an internal logic only they can navigate.

The stoic practice is not to copy someone else's environment. It is to understand your own brain well enough to design for it deliberately. That understanding comes from honest observation, not from what productivity books say a workspace should look like.

People as environment

Environment is not only physical. The people you spend time with are part of the environment your brain operates in. And for ADHD brains, the social environment has an outsized effect on functioning.

Accountability partners work for ADHD because the presence of another person activates a different motivational system than self-directed intention. Body doubling, the practice of working alongside someone else even without interaction, reduces procrastination for many people with ADHD in ways that solo effort cannot replicate.

The stoics understood this. They consistently recommended choosing your company carefully, not for social reasons, but because the people around you shape the quality of your thinking and the standards you hold yourself to.

> *"Associate with people who are likely to improve you. Welcome those who are capable of making you better."*
> **— Seneca, Letters to Lucilius**

Seneca is not being elitist. He is being precise. The people you spend the most time with are part of your cognitive and emotional environment. For an ADHD brain that is more responsive to external conditions than most, that is not a soft observation. It is a practical one.

YOUR PRACTICE
2-minute stoic exercises

Practice 16.1: The friction audit (10 minutes, once)

Walk through your most common daily failures, not the dramatic ones, the small recurring ones. For each one, ask:

- What makes this harder than it needs to be? What friction is in the way of the right behavior?
- What makes the unhelpful alternative easier? What friction is missing?

Then make one environmental change for each failure. Just one, per failure. Small and specific.

Example
Failure: I do not take my medication consistently. Friction analysis: it is in the medicine cabinet, which I do not always open in the morning. Change: move it next to the coffee maker, which I always use.

You are not changing your behavior. You are changing the conditions. The behavior often follows on its own.

Practice 16.2: The focus environment design (once)

Identify the one task or type of work that is most important to you and most consistently difficult to start. Then deliberately design the environment for that task.

1. What needs to be visible and accessible?
2. What needs to be removed or hidden?
3. What sound conditions work best for you?
4. What time of day is your initiation system most reliable?
5. Who, if anyone, helps you focus by being present?

Write down the answers. Then set up that environment once, properly. The setup cost is one hour. The return is every session of that work from now on starting under better conditions.

Practice 16.3: The body double experiment (this week)

Pick one task you have been consistently avoiding. Find a body double: someone who will sit with you, in person or on a video call, while you both work independently.

No conversation needed. No accountability check-in. Just the presence of another person while you work.

Try it once. Notice what happens to your ability to start and sustain the task. For most people with ADHD, the effect is immediate and surprising. The stoics would not be surprised at all.

CHAPTER 17

You Are Not Alone in This

Stoic cosmopolitanism, the late diagnosis experience, and the relief of belonging to a larger story

---

The stoics had a concept they called cosmopolitanism. It came from a simple observation: human beings are not only citizens of their city, their country, or their community. They are, in a deeper sense, citizens of the world. Members of a single human family.

The word cosmopolitan comes from two Greek roots: cosmos, meaning world or universe, and polites, meaning citizen. A cosmopolitan is a citizen of the universe.

For the stoics, this was not a poetic flourish. It was a claim with practical implications. If all human beings share the same fundamental nature, then you are never as alone as you feel. Whatever you are struggling with, someone else has struggled with it. Whatever makes you feel like an outlier, it has made others feel the same way.

For people with ADHD, especially those who spent years not knowing why they functioned differently from everyone around them, that idea can land with an unexpected force.

The late diagnosis experience

A significant proportion of adults with ADHD were not diagnosed in childhood. They went through school, through early adulthood, through careers and relationships, carrying a neurological difference that nobody named and nobody accommodated.

What they accumulated instead was a story. A story about why they were the way they were. Lazy. Flaky. Too much. Too emotional. Bright but not living up to their potential. Capable of more if they just applied themselves.

That story, told from the outside and eventually adopted from the inside, becomes part of how you understand yourself. And it is wrong. Not partially wrong. Fundamentally wrong in its framing. Because it attributes to character what is actually neurology.

When a late diagnosis arrives, it does something strange and important simultaneously. It explains the past. And it makes the past harder to look at, because you can now see clearly how much of the difficulty was unnecessary. How much of the shame was undeserved. How many of the verdicts were delivered without the relevant information.

That combination, relief and grief at once, is one of the most distinctive features of the late diagnosis experience. And it deserves to be named as such, not managed away, not rushed through, but genuinely acknowledged.

You are not behind
A late diagnosis does not mean you wasted those years. It means you navigated them without a map. That is not failure. That required a specific kind of resourcefulness that most people never develop, because they never had to.

What stoic cosmopolitanism offers

The cosmopolitan idea does several things for the person carrying the weight of a late ADHD diagnosis.

First, it places your experience in a larger context. You are not the only person who has gone decades without understanding why their mind works differently. Millions of people are carrying the same history. That does not erase your specific experience, but it does dissolve some of the isolation around it.

Second, it reframes the comparison problem. People with ADHD often compare their insides to other people's outsides, their inner chaos to other people's apparent competence, and find themselves consistently lacking. The cosmopolitan lens says: every person you are comparing yourself to is also carrying something. The appearance of ease is almost never the whole story.

Third, it points toward community. Not as a nice-to-have, but as a genuine resource for the ADHD brain. The stoics valued philosophical community, people who were working on the same things you are working on, as an essential part of the practice. For people with ADHD, community with others who share the experience is not just emotionally supportive. It is practically useful.

> *"We are all connected. To one another and to the larger whole of which we are a part. The philosophy that does not recognize this is incomplete."*
> **— Marcus Aurelius, Meditations**

The specific value of ADHD community

There is something that happens when people with ADHD find each other that does not happen in other contexts.

The strategies that work get shared without embarrassment. The patterns that cause shame get named with recognition instead of judgment. The failures that would be devastating to confess in a neurotypical context become, in a room full of people with ADHD, almost funny. Almost familiar. Almost a source of connection rather than isolation.

That shift is not trivial. It is the difference between carrying a difficulty alone and carrying it in company. The weight is the same. The experience of carrying it is completely different.

The stoics knew this. They practiced philosophy in groups. They wrote letters to each other. They commented on each other's progress and failures with a candor that only comes from shared commitment to the same work.

Finding your equivalent of that, the ADHD forum, the support group, the two friends who also have the diagnosis and will laugh with you about the thing you both did, is not optional self-care. It is infrastructure.

You are not your diagnosis

A necessary balance to everything in this chapter.

The stoic cosmopolitan move is to recognize shared humanity, not to reduce yourself to a category. You are a person with ADHD. You are not an ADHD person, as if the diagnosis were the sum of you.

The diagnosis explains certain patterns. It does not determine your character, your capacity, your relationships, or your future. The stoics were very clear that what you are made of, your fundamental nature as a rational and social being, is not reducible to your circumstances or your difficulties.

You share something with millions of other people. You are also completely singular. Both of those things are true. The cosmopolitan idea holds both without collapsing one into the other.

> *"Confine yourself to the present."*
> — **Marcus Aurelius, Meditations**

That instruction, in this context, means: do not let the past diagnosis, the years without it, the accumulated history, collapse into the present moment as if it determines what happens next. The past is fixed. The present is where you actually live. And the present, for anyone willing to work with it honestly, is still open.

YOUR PRACTICE
2-minute stoic exercises

Practice 17.1: The rewrite (2 minutes)

Think of one story you tell about yourself that was formed before you understood your ADHD. A story about why you are the way you are that uses the wrong framing: lazy, careless, incapable.

Now rewrite it with the right framing. Not a flattering version. An accurate one.

Example

Old story: I never finished anything I started because I lacked discipline. Rewritten: I consistently lost momentum on projects because my dopamine system requires novelty and visible progress to sustain engagement. I was not failing. I was running the wrong fuel in the wrong engine.

Write the rewritten version somewhere you will see it. Not as a mantra. As a correction to the record.

Practice 17.2: Find one person (this week)

Find one person who also has ADHD, or who is working on understanding their own brain, and have one honest conversation with them about something in this book.

Not a support group necessarily. Not a formal arrangement. Just one conversation, with one person, about one thing you recognized in yourself while reading.

The stoics practiced philosophy in pairs before they practiced it in groups. The conversation is the practice. It does not need to be a program.

Practice 17.3: The cosmopolitan reminder (as needed)

When you feel most alone in your experience, most like an outlier, most like everyone else is managing something that you cannot, try one sentence:

Say this

Someone, right now, is sitting with exactly what I am sitting with. I am not the first. I am not the last. I am not alone in this.

This is not a comfort. It is a fact. The stoics built their entire social philosophy on facts like this. Not because facts dissolve difficulty, but because accurate facts create a more stable ground to stand on than the distorted ones the isolated mind tends to generate.

You are a citizen of a larger world than the one inside your head. That world includes a great many people who know exactly what this feels like.

CHAPTER 18

Relationships That Survive ADHD

Oikeíosis, the stoic circle of care, and how to be in relationship without shame or pretense

---

The stoics had a concept called oikeíosis, which roughly translates as appropriation or affiliation. It describes the natural human tendency to feel connected to, and responsible for, the people around us.

The idea was that this tendency starts with the self and expands outward: first to your immediate family, then to your extended community, then to humanity at large. Not equally at every level. But present at all of them.

For people with ADHD, the relational world is often complicated in specific ways. Not because the capacity for connection is absent. It is frequently very strong. But because the features of ADHD that create difficulty in other areas also create difficulty in relationships: the emotional intensity, the inconsistent follow-through, the time blindness, the impulsivity, the hyperfocus that can make someone feel central and then the loss of interest that makes them feel dropped.

This chapter is about what the stoic framework offers for navigating those complications honestly.

The ADHD relational patterns worth knowing

Before we get to the philosophy, it helps to name the patterns clearly. Because relationships are where a lot of ADHD shame lives, and shame thrives on vagueness.

The most common ADHD relational difficulties in adults are not dramatic. They are cumulative.

6. Forgetting things that matter to the other person, even when you genuinely care about them.
7. Showing up inconsistently: intensely present sometimes, apparently absent at others.
8. Interrupting, finishing sentences, or moving to a new topic before the other person feels heard.
9. Struggling to follow through on commitments that seemed completely manageable when you made them.
10. Reacting more strongly than the situation warranted and then recovering faster than the other person can.
11. Hyperfocusing on a new relationship at the start and then, once the novelty settles, struggling to maintain the same intensity.

None of these are character defects. They are the behavioral expression of specific executive function challenges in a relational context. That does not make them consequence-free. But it does make them understandable, and understandable is where change becomes possible.

The important distinction

Understanding why you do something does not excuse the impact on others. It gives you the information you need to address it honestly rather than managing it through shame, which never works for long.

What the stoics asked of us in relationships

The stoic view of relationships was grounded in duty and genuine care, not in performance or reputation management.

Epictetus was direct about this: your relationships require you to show up as the best version of what you are, not as a performance of someone else's idea of what you should be. And showing up honestly includes being honest about your limitations.

For people with ADHD, that means something specific. It means telling the people you are close to how your brain works, not as an excuse delivered after the damage, but as information shared before it, so that the people who matter to you can understand what they are actually dealing with.

That conversation is not easy. It requires vulnerability that many adults with ADHD have learned to avoid, because the early experiences of being honest about their struggles were not always received well. But it is the only alternative to a relationship built on the exhausting fiction that you function the way other people expect you to.

> *"He who is not capable of taking care of himself cannot take care of others. But taking care of yourself first does not mean ignoring others. It means being honest about what you have to give."*
>
> — **Epictetus, Discourses**

The ADHD conversation worth having

At some point in any close relationship, the ADHD conversation becomes necessary. Not a comprehensive medical briefing. A human conversation about how you function and what that means for the other person.

The stoic version of this conversation has three parts, and they are worth thinking about before you have it.

The first part is accurate description. Not catastrophizing, not minimizing. What is actually true about how your ADHD shows up in this relationship? What patterns does the other person probably already recognize, even if they have not named them?

The second part is genuine accountability. What impact have those patterns had? Not defensively, not with extended apology, but with honest acknowledgment of the effect on the other person.

The third part is specific commitment. Not I will try to be better, which is a commitment to a feeling rather than an action. But one specific thing you are working on, and one specific thing you are asking for.

That third part is the hardest and the most important. Because it converts the conversation from a confession into a collaboration. And collaboration is where relationships actually improve.

Asking for what you need

People with ADHD often find it difficult to ask for what they need in relationships. Partly because the shame history makes need feel like weakness. Partly because years of failing to meet expectations have made asking feel presumptuous.

The stoics had a clear position on this. Asking for what you genuinely need, in an honest and specific way, is not weakness. It is the natural expression of being in relationship with another person. It is also, practically, the only way to get your needs met without either suffering in silence or creating the resentment that comes from expecting others to guess.

What do you actually need from the people close to you? Not in general. Specifically.

More patience with inconsistent timing? Reminders delivered without judgment? The space to move around while having a serious conversation? Someone who checks in rather than waiting for you to reach out? Someone who does not interpret silence as indifference?

Those are reasonable things to ask for. And the people who genuinely care about you would rather know them than spend years misinterpreting the ADHD patterns.

The oikeíosis expansion

The stoics taught that genuine care for others expands from those closest to us outward. And they were clear that this expansion requires ongoing attention, not just good intentions.

For ADHD, whose relational energy is often uneven, that expansion does not have to be consistent in intensity. It has to be consistent in intention. The difference between forgetting a friend's birthday and not caring about the friend is real and important. One is an executive function failure. The other is a values failure.

Your relationships can absorb executive function failures, especially when they are understood and addressed honestly.

What they struggle to absorb is the sense that they do not matter.

Making sure the people you care about know they matter to you, in whatever form of communication works for your brain, is the stoic relational practice. Not perfectly. Not constantly. But with enough consistency that the intention is clear, even when the execution is imperfect.

> *"Wherever there is a human being, there is an opportunity for kindness."*
> — **Seneca, On the Happy Life**

YOUR PRACTICE
2-minute stoic exercises

Practice 18.1: The honest relationship inventory (2 minutes)

Pick one relationship that matters to you and where ADHD has created some friction. Write down three things:

- One specific pattern that has caused difficulty in this relationship.
- What the impact of that pattern has probably been on the other person.
- One specific thing you could do or say this week to address it directly.

Not a grand gesture. One specific thing. The stoics were practical about repair. Small, honest, specific actions build more trust over time than large dramatic ones.

Practice 18.2: The ADHD conversation (when ready)

With one person who is close to you, have a version of the three-part conversation described in this chapter.

- This is how my ADHD actually shows up in this relationship. Specific, honest, no dramatization.
- The impact that has probably had on you. Acknowledged without defensive explanation.
- One thing I am working on. One thing I am asking for from you.

You do not have to do all three parts in one conversation. Start with one. The stoics valued the conversation over the performance of it. An honest partial conversation is worth more than a perfect one that never happens.

Practice 18.3: The consistent signal (ongoing)

Choose one person you care about. Choose one small, recurring action that communicates to them that they matter, something that fits your brain and requires no planning to maintain.

Examples

A voice message instead of a text, because it feels more like you. A specific question you ask every time you talk. A standing plan that does not require coordination, because coordination is where ADHD drops things.

The consistency matters more than the size of the gesture. A small reliable signal over months says more than an occasional large one. This is oikeíosis made practical: the circle of care, maintained not by intensity but by intention.

CHAPTER 19

Duty Without Self-Destruction

Kathêkon, chronic guilt, and the difference between genuine obligation and the weight you never agreed to carry

---

The stoics had a concept called kathêkon. It is usually translated as appropriate action or duty, though neither translation quite captures it.

Kathêkon means the action that is fitting for who you are, in the circumstances you are actually in. Not the action that would be fitting for an idealized version of you. Not the action that would be fitting for someone with different constraints. The action that is genuinely appropriate for this person, with this nature, in this situation.

For people with ADHD, that distinction is not academic. It is the difference between a life organized around genuine responsibility and a life organized around guilt for not meeting obligations that were never honestly yours to meet.

The chronic guilt problem

Guilt, in appropriate doses, is functional. It signals that you have done something that conflicts with your values. It motivates repair. It maintains your integrity in relationship to other people.

Chronic guilt, the kind that runs continuously regardless of what you are actually doing, is different. It is not a signal anymore. It is background noise. And for people with ADHD, it is extremely common.

It comes from decades of missing things, forgetting things, failing to meet expectations that seemed reasonable to everyone except the person with ADHD who was working twice as hard just to get halfway there. It comes from the accumulated weight of promises made in good faith and broken by a brain that could not reliably deliver what the mouth committed to.

Over time, this chronic guilt stops being about specific failures. It becomes a general orientation. A sense that you owe more than you are giving, in every direction, at all times. That everyone around you is being shortchanged by your existence.

That is not an accurate perception. It is what happens when a sensitive, self-aware brain has processed years of unrealistic expectation without a framework for distinguishing genuine obligation from borrowed shame.

The distinction that matters

Genuine guilt says: I did something specific that conflicted with my values. Here is what I can do to address it. Chronic guilt says: I am, in general, not enough. It offers no specific action because it is not about a specific failure. It is about identity. And it is wrong.

What kathêkon actually asks

The stoic concept of appropriate action starts with an honest assessment of who you are and what you are actually capable of. Not what you could theoretically do on a perfect day. What you can reliably do, from your actual starting point, with your actual brain, in your actual circumstances.

Epictetus was very clear about this. He did not believe in obligations that exceeded a person's genuine capacity. He believed that what was required of you was a function of what was actually available to you. A person who is sick is not obligated to perform at the level of someone who is well. A person whose executive functions are challenged is not obligated to deliver the same kind of consistent output as a person whose executive functions are not.

That does not mean lowering standards. It means calibrating them honestly. Which is a harder thing than either lowering or raising them, because it requires looking clearly at the gap between what you want to give and what you can reliably give, and being honest about both.

> *"Do what nature requires. Set out immediately if possible. Do not look around to see if people will know about it. Do not expect Plato's ideal state, but be satisfied with even the smallest step forward."*
> — **Marcus Aurelius, Meditations**

The smallest step forward. Not the complete transformation. Not the perfect performance. The thing that is genuinely possible right now, from where you actually are.

For a brain that tends to oscillate between all-or-nothing, between the fantasy of total change and the paralysis of feeling unable to change at all, that instruction is worth reading more than once.

Obligations you never agreed to

One of the most useful things the stoic framework does is help you identify which obligations are genuine and which were assigned to you by someone else's expectations without your actual consent.

People with ADHD often carry a very heavy load of the second kind. The obligation to function the way neurotypical people function. The obligation to meet deadlines with the same ease as people whose time perception is reliable. The obligation to sustain attention on demand. The obligation to remember things that neurotypical working memory holds easily.

None of those are genuine obligations. They are expectations built on a false assumption about your neurology. You did not agree to them. You simply could not meet them, and then absorbed the guilt for the failure as if it were your fault that the expectation was wrong.

The stoic move is to sort those out. Not to abandon all responsibility. To be precise about which responsibilities are genuinely yours and which are expectations you inherited from a world that did not understand how your brain works.

That sorting is uncomfortable. It requires saying, sometimes out loud, that some of what you have been feeling guilty about was never yours to carry. And that can feel presumptuous or defensive, especially if you have been carrying it for a very long time.

It is neither. It is accuracy. And accuracy is where genuine responsibility, the kind that actually holds and actually improves things, begins.

What you do owe

After the sorting, what is left?

You owe honesty. About your limitations, your patterns, your failures when they happen.

You owe genuine effort. Not perfect execution, but the real attempt to do what you said you would do, and the honest acknowledgment when you cannot.

You owe repair. When your ADHD patterns cause harm to people you care about, you owe the work of making it right, not through extended self-punishment, but through specific and honest action.

You owe continued growth. Not perfection. The ongoing practice of working with your brain rather than against it, building systems, asking for help, trying again after failure.

That is a real set of obligations. And it is enough. Not more than enough. Enough.

The stoics called the person who meets their genuine obligations a good person, not a perfect one. The bar was never perfection. It was honest effort in the right direction.

That bar, you can meet. You may already be meeting it, while simultaneously carrying guilt for the obligations that were never yours.

Put those down. They were not yours to begin with.

YOUR PRACTICE

2-minute stoic exercises

Practice 19.1: The guilt sort (2 minutes)

Write down the three things you feel most guilty about in your life right now. Then, for each one, answer one question:

> **The sorting question**
> Is this guilt about something I genuinely did that conflicted with my values? Or is it about failing to meet an expectation that was built on a false picture of what I can reliably do?

If it is the first: what is the one specific action that addresses it? Do that.

If it is the second: name the expectation, name why it was unrealistic, and practice setting it down. Not once. As many times as it comes back.

Practice 19.2: The genuine obligation list (2 minutes)

Write down your actual obligations. Not everything you feel you should do. The things you have genuinely committed to and that matter to the people involved.

Then look at the list and ask: is this realistic? Can I actually deliver this, consistently, from my actual starting point?

If the answer is no: which obligation needs to be renegotiated, reduced, or handed off? Have that conversation this week. Honest renegotiation is not failure. Silently failing to meet an unrealistic commitment is.

Practice 19.3: The enough statement (daily)

At the end of each day this week, write or say one sentence:

Today I did what I genuinely could. That was enough for today.

Not every day will feel like enough. Say it anyway. The stoics practiced statements of accurate orientation, not statements of feeling. Over time, the accurate statement shapes the feeling, not the other way around.

You are not being asked to believe it immediately. You are being asked to practice it. That is how all stoic practice works. The belief follows the repetition, slowly and reliably, like every other thing worth building.

CHAPTER 20

A Philosophy That Does Not Ask You to Be Someone Else

Integrating the practice, designing your minimum daily philosophy, and what comes next

---

We have covered a great deal of ground.

We started with Marcus Aurelius arguing with himself in a military tent at dawn. We moved through the myths about stoicism, through the neuroscience of ADHD, through the dichotomy of control and the distracted pilot and the problem of impulses and the question of how to meditate when you cannot sit still.

We spent time with rejection and shame and anger and time blindness. With loving how you function and planning for failure and pre-deciding your values and designing your environment and finding your people and navigating your relationships and sorting your genuine obligations from the borrowed guilt.

That is a lot of material. And if you have ADHD, there is a reasonable chance that some of it landed clearly and some of it slipped past and some of it you will not remember by next week.

That is fine. That is how ADHD works. And that is why this chapter exists.

You do not need all of it

The stoics were not building a system that required complete mastery before it became useful. They were building a set of tools, each of which could be used independently, each of which offered something of value on its own.

Marcus Aurelius returned to the same ideas over and over across decades of writing, not because he had never understood them, but because understanding them was not the same as living them. The practice was the return. Always the return.

You do not need to have absorbed every chapter equally. You do not need to be applying every practice simultaneously. What you need is one or two ideas that actually changed something in how you think about your brain, and one or two practices that you will actually do.

That is enough. That is, in fact, exactly enough.

> *"Perfection of character is this: to live each day as if it were your last, without frenzy, without apathy, without pretense."*
> **— Marcus Aurelius, Meditations**

Without pretense. That is the phrase that matters most for people with ADHD. Not the performance of a kind of functioning you do not have. Not the exhausting fiction that you work the way other people expect you to work. An honest, daily engagement with the brain you actually have, bringing to it whatever tools have proven useful.

Your minimum daily philosophy

The stoics had morning practices and evening practices and midday checkpoints. For most people with ADHD, a full stoic daily routine is both appealing and entirely unsustainable.

So let us be realistic. What is the minimum that actually makes a difference?

Research on habit formation and ADHD consistently suggests that anchor habits, small practices attached to existing routines, are more durable than standalone practices. The question is not what your ideal daily philosophy would look like. It is what your minimum sustainable one looks like, attached to things you already do.

> **A realistic minimum**
> Morning: one question, thirty seconds. What is the one thing that might be hard today, and what quality do I want to bring to it? Evening: one question, sixty seconds. Where did I return to myself today, even once? As needed: one tool from whichever chapter applies to what is happening right now.

That is the whole practice. Two minutes total, anchored to existing routine, with a toolkit available for harder moments.

If you do that consistently, you will have a stoic practice. It will not look like Marcus Aurelius's practice. It will look like yours. Which is the only practice that will last.

What changes and what does not

Let us be honest about what this book can and cannot do.

It cannot change your neurology. ADHD is real, it is neurological, and it will continue to shape how your brain works regardless of how much philosophy you read or practice.

What it can change is your relationship to that neurology. The story you tell about it. The amount of energy you spend fighting it versus working with it. The quality of the internal conversation you have when things go wrong. The speed with which you return after a drift. The precision with which you understand your own patterns. The honesty with which you show up in your relationships and your work.

Those changes are not small. They compound. A slightly more accurate inner narrative, practiced daily, produces a significantly different life over years. Not because the ADHD disappears. Because you stop spending most of your energy on a fight you were never going to win, and start spending it on a life you can actually build.

The practice is the return

Every chapter in this book has been about some version of the same move.

You drift. You notice. You return.

Your attention drifts and you bring it back. Your emotions spike and you create a pause. Your impulses pull you somewhere and you ask what they are actually saying. Your inner critic runs and you check whether it is telling you something useful. Your time dissolves and you reconnect to what matters. Your obligations pile up and you sort the real from the borrowed. Your relationships fray and you repair them honestly.

Every single one of those is a return. And the return is not a failure to have stayed on course. It is the practice. It is, quite literally, what you are training.

Marcus Aurelius returned to the same reminders for decades. Epictetus taught the same ideas his entire adult life, to students who needed to hear them again. Seneca wrote letter after letter covering the same terrain, because living a philosophy requires more repetition than understanding it does.

You will drift from this. That is guaranteed. You will have weeks where none of the practices happen and the internal critic runs unchallenged and the impulses win and the relationships suffer and the guilt piles back up.

And then you will return. Because the return is available to you at any moment. It does not require having maintained an unbroken streak. It does not require being in a particular state. It just requires noticing, and choosing, one more time.

That is the whole practice. It was always the whole practice.

A final word on being this kind of person

You have a brain that works differently from most of the brains around you. That difference has cost you things. Real things. Time, opportunity, relationships, energy, and years of carrying a story about yourself that was built on wrong information.

It has also given you things. Not as compensation. Not as a silver lining that makes the difficulty acceptable. Just as part of the full picture of what it is to be you.

The stoics did not believe in idealized people. They believed in actual people, working honestly with what they had, trying to do what was genuinely right, failing sometimes, returning always.

You are exactly the kind of person this philosophy was built for. Not because ADHD makes you special. Because you are a human being working with the mind you actually have, in the life you actually have, trying to do it with some honesty and some grace.

That is all any of the stoics were ever doing.

That is all this is.

YOUR PRACTICE
2-minute stoic exercises

Practice 20.1: Your one page (2 minutes)

From everything in this book, write down:

- The one idea that changed something in how you understand your brain.
- The one practice you will actually keep doing.
- The one sentence that best describes what you want your relationship with your own mind to look like.

One page. Or less. This is your personal philosophy, stripped to its minimum. Keep it somewhere visible. Not to follow it perfectly. To return to it when you drift.

Practice 20.2: The anchor habit (set it once)

Choose your two anchor moments: morning and evening. Attach one stoic question to each.

Morning: what is the one thing that might be hard today, and what quality do I want to bring to it?

Evening: where did I return to myself today, even once?

Decide exactly when you will do each one. Not a general intention. A specific moment. While the coffee brews. While brushing your teeth. In the first minute after getting into bed.

Specific moment plus specific question equals a practice that can actually survive an ADHD brain. Vague intention plus general aspiration equals a practice that will not.

Practice 20.3: The return promise (once, to yourself)

Write this down, in your own words, and mean it:

> **The promise**
> When I drift from this, which I will, I will return. Not perfectly. Not immediately. But I will return. The drift is not the failure. Not returning would be. And I have already proven I am someone who returns.

You have. You read this book. You returned to it across chapters, across days, across the drifts that happened between sessions. That is evidence.

The stoics believed that evidence mattered more than aspiration. Here is yours: you kept coming back.

That is the practice. Keep doing it.

EPILOGUE

The Sky Was Always There

A final word for the brain that kept reading

You made it here.

That might sound like a small thing. It is not.

If you have ADHD, finishing a book is not a given. Finishing a book that asks you to examine your own patterns, sit with difficult history, and try new things while you read, that requires something specific. Not discipline. Something better than discipline.

It requires caring enough to keep returning.

And you did.

I want to tell you something directly, without the structure of chapters or practices or callout boxes.

The years you spent not knowing why you worked differently were not wasted. I know it can feel that way. The diagnosis that came late, the systems that failed, the relationships that strained, the opportunities that slipped past while you were busy trying to be someone your brain was never built to be. That is real loss and it deserves to be acknowledged.

But here is what is also true.

You navigated every one of those years without the map. You built your own workarounds, your own rhythms, your own ways of getting through. Some of them were brilliant. Some of them were exhausting. All of them were yours. And the resourcefulness that produced them did not disappear when the diagnosis arrived. It became available to you more consciously.

That is not nothing. That is, in fact, a great deal.

> *"You have power over your mind, not outside events. Realize this, and you will find strength."*
> **— Marcus Aurelius, Meditations**

Marcus Aurelius wrote those words to himself. Not to posterity. To the man in the tent who was struggling to get up, who had to argue himself into the day, who kept drifting and kept returning for twenty years on the throne of the most powerful empire in the world.

He was not serene. He was committed. And there is a kind of strength in commitment that serenity does not touch, because commitment does not depend on how you feel. It depends on what you choose, again and again, in the small moments that add up to a life.

You have a brain that makes some of those moments harder than they are for most people. You also have something that is genuinely rare: the capacity to feel things with full intensity, to make connections that linear thinking misses, to care about things with a depth that other people sometimes find alarming and often find invaluable.

The stoics would not ask you to mute any of that. They would ask you to work with it honestly. To stop pretending it is not there. To stop apologizing for it to people who were working from the wrong map. To start building, deliberately and without shame, a life that fits the brain you actually have.

That life is possible. Not perfect. Not without difficulty. Not without the drifts and the returns and the occasional spectacular failure that requires honest repair.

But possible. Genuinely, specifically, for-you possible.

You are not behind. You are not broken. You are not too late.

You are someone with a particular kind of mind, equipped now with a particular set of tools, standing at the beginning of a practice that will look different every day and improve, slowly and then noticeably, over time.

The stoics believed that the examined life, lived honestly and with genuine effort toward what is good, is available to every person regardless of their circumstances. Not easily. Not without cost. But available.

To you. Right now. As you are.

In chapter six, we used an image: the mind as a sky, and thoughts and emotions as the weather passing through. The storm arrives. The storm passes. The sky was always there.

That sky is yours. The storms will keep coming. They always do.

But you know now what the sky is. And you know how to find it again.

By the way, you are wonderful.

www.ingramcontent.com/pod-product-compliance
Lightning Source LLC
Chambersburg PA
CBHW041302210926
51847CB00010B/114
9789189876682